TEENAGE MARRIAGES

TEENAGE MARRIAGES
A Demographic Analysis

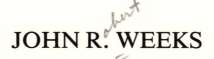

JOHN R. WEEKS

INTERNATIONAL POPULATION AND URBAN RESEARCH
UNIVERSITY OF CALIFORNIA, BERKELEY

Studies in Population and Urban Demography, Number 2

GREENWOOD PRESS
WESTPORT CONNECTICUT • LONDON ENGLAND

Library of Congress Cataloging in Publication Data

Weeks, John Robert, 1944-
    Teenage marriages.

    (Studies in population and urban demography ; no. 2)
    Bibliography: p.
    Includes index.
    1. Teen-age marriage—United States. 2. Teenage marriage—
California. I. Title. II. Series.
HQ799.2.M3W44   301.42   76-5330
ISBN 0-8371-8898-9

Library of Congress Catalog Card Number: 76-5330
ISBN: 0-8371-8898-9

First published in 1976

Greenwood Press, a division of Williamhouse-Regency Inc.
51 Riverside Avenue, Westport, Connecticut 06880

Printed in the United States of America

CONTENTS

00151

FIGURES

TABLES

FOREWORD

In advanced societies, adolescence is a paradoxical part of the life cycle. A time of freedom and exuberance, it is also a period of tragic mistakes. With parental control slipping, with nobody else taking overall responsibility, and yet with the adolescent unable to guide his own development satisfactorily, the teenage years are a time of lost opportunities, of doors closed on the basis of whims, ignorance, and rebellion—a time of decisions regretted later in life.

Not the least paradoxical is the reproductive power that biology gives to the teenager. Although the creation of new human beings is serious business—more serious than almost anything else—it is often done by those too young to drink in a bar, see a pornographic movie, take a responsible job, or even drop out of school. In the United States in 1970, for example, 235,342 births were to girls aged 12 to 17. These were 6.3 percent of all births in that year.

To fathom the consequences of immature child-bearing requires hard information. It particularly requires longitudinal data tracing the pathway from teenage pregnancy to subsequent outcomes. The present study has provided important findings of this type. Taking advantage of the anonymous, computerized record-linkage system made possible through a joint project between our research office at the University of California and the California State Department of Health, the author, Professor John Weeks, has traced in the registration system the births and divorces arising from the marriages of teenagers in 1966. Using the information on these records, he has thrown much light on the fate of the couples and their infants.

His findings show that teenagers who marry and their off-spring are at a disadvantage. For instance, some 60 percent of first births to women married at age 15 were conceived prior to marriage, whereas only 11 percent of those to women married at age 21 were so conceived. Similarly, the more youthful the husband, the more likely was the marriage to be the sequel to pregnancy. But even births conceived after marriage came faster to individuals married in their teens than to those married later. Infant mortality was substantially higher among children born of very young mothers and among those premaritally conceived. Finally, as one would expect from the number of young marriages induced by pregnancy or other adverse circumstances, the probability of divorce was much higher for teenage than for later marriages, and higher still when the first child was conceived premaritally.

Doubtless teenage reproductive behavior will change. Indeed, it has already changed since 1966. Teenage marriages have declined, but teenage child-bearing has not decreased commensurately. As a result, the ratio of illegitimate births among teenagers has risen dramatically. The basic problem is evidently not teenage marriage per se, but teenage child-bearing. The particular period that the present study documents is therefore a segment of a trend of major significance for contemporary society.

The project that enabled the author to obtain his data was supported by the National Institute of Child Health and Human Development (NIH-N01-HD-32728). We are grateful for that support and for the analysis that Professor Weeks has made of the material. It is our pleasure to include the volume in the Studies in Population and Urban Demography series.

—Kingsley Davis

International Population and Urban Research
Institute of International Studies
University of California, Berkeley
April 14, 1976

PREFACE

This study was initiated in 1970 as part of a larger program of investigation into fertility and family formation at International Population and Urban Research (IPUR), University of California, Berkeley. Dr. Kingsley Davis, Director of IPUR, suggested that I undertake a record linkage of marriages, births, and divorces in California to generate data for analysis in my doctoral dissertation in the Department of Demography at Berkeley. The original record linkage data, reported in 1972 in that dissertation—*A Demographic Analysis of Teenage Marriages*—linked marriages in California in 1966 with births for 1965 through 1968, and dissolutions from 1966-1969.

In the summer of 1972 I returned to IPUR to revise and to improve the accuracy of the record linkage of marriages and births, concentrating entirely on matching 1966 marriages in California to 1966-1967 births. All of the data discussed in this monograph refer to data generated in this more recent record linkage. As I note in the Appendixes, however, the record linkage methodology remains imperfect. Work is still continuing on various aspects of the linkage system, and reports on the data resulting from these improvements in the information system will be forthcoming. The statistical analysis has been kept as simple as possible. I feel that unduly elaborate statistical manipulation of data abounds in the social sciences today, frequently to the detriment of the reader's ability, or willingness, to understand the substantive points being made. I have tried to avoid what I believe to be an error in that direction and have almost always limited the analysis to rates and to explications of frequency distributions.

The reader is also spared a detailed discussion of record linkage methodology in the substantive chapters, one through nine. Instead, this material is included as Appendixes. It is my hope that with this analysis of early marital fertility and dissolution adding new and useful insights into the demography of teenage marriages, we can then lay the groundwork for analyses of the sociological processes operating to produce teenage fertility.

This study was made possible through the cooperation of several people and agencies. Financially, the research was supported in part by training grants to the Department of Demography from the National Center for Health Services Research and Development (8 T01HS00059) and from the Ford Foundation. Research was also supported by a contract from the National Institute of Child Health and Human Development, for which Dr. Kingsley Davis is the principal investigator. To Dr. Davis who has guided my intellectual development and academic career since my undergraduate days at Berkeley, my debt is too enormous to be expressed in a list of acknowledgments. Throughout, his advice has been sought and heeded. In addition, I have benefited from the very fine editing of Jan Seibert.

I am also grateful to the California State Department of Public Health for making available to me the computer tape files used in this record linkage project, and for cooperating so fully with my research efforts. Beth Berkov deserves special mention for her coordination of certain aspects of this research.

Dr. Edwin Jackson, Paul Shipley, Roger Smith, Harry Green-blatt, Yvonne Bristol, and Yosh Yemene, all of the California Department of Public Health, also provided valuable assistance.

Brief expressions of thanks only scratch the surface of my gratitude to the persons named above, and are even less ade-quate for my wife, Deanna. Her endurance, encouragement, and assistance throughout have been truly phenomenal and inspirational.

J.R.W.
San Diego
September 1975

1

TEENAGE MARRIAGES: HOW AND WHY WE ANALYZE THEM

Thousands of teenagers marry every year in the United States. In fact, teenage marriages are more common in the United States than in almost any other part of the industrialized world. It is a wealthy country, so early marriages are tolerated, sometimes even encouraged, but at what price? For the teenage couple, marriage may be important as an exciting entry into adulthood, but for many parents of teenage brides and grooms, for family counselors, for divorce lawyers, educators, and politicians, teenage marriages are important because of the surplus of problems with which they are associated. These problems all too frequently turn excitement into turmoil for the teenagers themselves. Premarital pregnancies, unhealthy children, infant mortality, economic insecurity, and divorce are some of the more prominent problems whose social implications make teenage marriages a vitally important topic for analysis.

What are the social and demographic implications of teenage marriages? A teenage marriage may short-circuit a woman's chance to develop a role alternate to that of housewifery and motherhood. The more teenage women who are married, the more pressure there will be for family-building activity, and the more important will be the other social problems associated with teenage marriages.

The crux of the question of early marriage lies in the birth of children. If no children were born, no health problems associated with children of young mothers would develop. If no children were born, divorce would create no difficulties in the maintenance, socialization, and social placement of children. If no children were born, no contribution would be made by teenage marriages to the nation's birth rate.

Marriage contributes to the problem of fertility by providing a socially acceptable outlet for childbearing, and being an inherently pronatalist institution in which the young bride and mother finds encouragement and reinforcement for continued childbearing. But even if no children are born immediately, teenage marriages may have dubious consequences. They may interrupt or cut off a teenager's chance for more education, a better job, and perhaps an input into increasing the quality of life in American society. Options are particularly foreclosed if the girl does not work, thus forcing the boy to work to support the pair. If the marriage effects a break between the teenagers and their parents, financial support for continuing an education may be shut off.

Let us examine in more detail some of the problems associated with early marriage. Premarital conceptions account for a high proportion of the early marital births to teenagers. According to the 1964-1966 National Natality Survey, 61 percent of the births to teenagers during the first year of marriage occurred within the first eight months, suggesting a premarital conception. For women aged 20-24 the percentage of births during the first year of marriage which were apparently conceived premaritally was 41 percent; for women aged 25-29 it was 22 percent; for women aged 30-34 it was 11 percent; and for women aged 35-44 it was 14 percent. Teenage brides, then, are much more likely than older women to be pregnant on their wedding day.

A large study in England, reported by Heady and Morris [1959], indicated that the incidence of stillbirth and particularly of mortality during the first six months of life is higher for children of mothers under 20 than for mothers who are in the 20-30 age range. A related study by Donnelly *et al.* [1960] showed that perinatal mortality (infant deaths during the first week of life) is associated with prematurity and toxemia, both of which are frequently associated with inadequate prenatal care, this perhaps being a general characteristic of teenage pregnancies. Stewart [1959] reported that stillbirths and neonatal (newborn) deaths were almost twice as frequent among premaritally as among postmaritally conceived births. Since most premarital conceptions are to teenagers, the problem socially, if not biologically, is age-related. Ashley [1968] has substantiated earlier findings that perinatal mortality is highest in those social classes in Britain in which teenage marriages are more frequent. In summarizing Yerushalmy's Hawaiian study, Day [1967] notes that postnatal infant mortality is highest for children born to women under age 20, but that younger women are least at risk of having fetal deaths, the latter echoing findings by Robinson [1967] and Israel and Wontersz [1963]. Immature live births are reported more frequently for teenagers than for older women [National Center for Health Statistics, 1970b]. New data on the mortality of children born to teenage women in California are analyzed in Chapter Seven.

A greater-than-average likelihood of marital dissolution is another important social consequence of early marriage. A United States Census Bureau sample of women married during 1960-1966, in which the incidence of divorce during the first two years of marriage was ascertained, showed that the chances of divorce early in marriage were nearly twice as high for wives married when they were under 18 as for women married between the ages of 18-19, and more than four times as high as for wives married when they were age 25 or older [U.S. Bureau of Census, 1971a].

Many writers have theorized that youthful marriages are frequently contracted with overly optimistic expectations regarding emotional and financial security [see for example, Bartz and Nye, 1970]. They are sometimes the consequence of early courtship involving an early loosening of parental control, early involvement with the opposite sex, and a resultant lowering of priorities given to such goals as education and career [Moss, 1965]. Teenage marriages are also resorted to as socially acceptable escape mechanisms from an unhappy home life. The search for happiness in a new relationship leads to premature legal adulthood and quick loss of unreasonably high expectations. Premarital pregnancy itself tends to lead to rapid disillusionment and early divorce. The discovery of pregnancy is a frequent precursor of marriage among the young—a means of becoming trapped into marriage or at least a result of impulsiveness or ignorance. When a pregnant woman marries, the chances of her marriage failing are considerably higher than for the bride not so burdened. For example, Christensen [1963a] in a study in Utah, found that in marriages in which a baby was born within six months after the wedding, 27 percent of the marriages had failed, whereas among marriages in which the first birth occurred no sooner than a year after marriage, approximately 5 percent of the marriages had failed (data were adjusted for marital duration).

Although as with all divorces, those among young women represent a problem of social reorganization, they are less likely than in the past to represent a substantial disruption in the overall fertility performance of the women involved. The reason for this, of course, is the high rate of remarriage. Jacobson [1959] and Goode [1956] have argued that the younger the divorcee, the more attractive will she be in the marriage market, and thus the shorter will be her time between marriages. Gebhard [1971] has added that around 75 percent of women whose marriages have ended in divorce have coitus during the interim period before their next marriage, and that among women getting divorced, those who engaged in pre-marital sexual activity will more than likely engage in post-marital sexual activity. The result, as Lauriat [1969] has shown, is that remarried women tend to catch up over time with continuously married women in terms of completed fertility.

These problems make it of practical importance to study teenage marriages. The purpose of this book, then, is to study the trends in and causes of teenage marriages and their associated phenomena. This is accomplished by a thorough review of the literature and by an analysis of new data from a linkage of marriage, birth, and divorce records in California. These data were generated as part of a larger study undertaken by International Population and Urban Research at the University of California, Berkeley, entitled "Family Formation and Fertility: Key Trends and Patterns," a project funded by the National Institute of Child Health and Human Development (Kingsley Davis, principal investigator). California was chosen as a case study since its demographic experience tends to mirror the rest of the nation, and since the California Department of Public Health was willing to cooperate in providing the raw data required for the linkage of vital statistics records.

CALIFORNIA COMPARED TO THE UNITED STATES

Figure 1 shows that the proportion of teenagers married in California generally has followed the pattern in the United States. In fact, California tends to exaggerate national trends, dropping lower or rising higher than United States lows and highs. The same similarities are observable with respect to changes in age at marriage over time (see Table 1). The average age at marriage has been increasing in the United States since 1959 [U.S. Bureau of Census, 1971a] and the same is true for California.

Although this study is an analysis of teenage marriages generally, the new data generated for this study refer specifically to women in the marriage cohort of 1966 in California—the women whose first marriage occurred in 1966 and in California. Let me now discuss the record linkage system which generated these data.

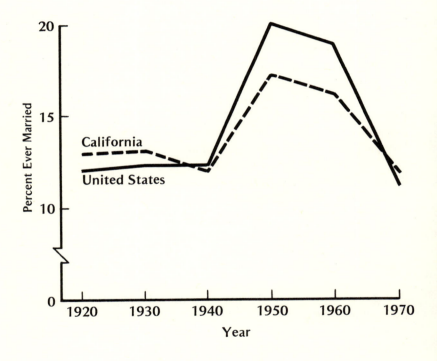

Figure 1

PERCENTAGES OF TEENAGERS WHO ARE EVER-MARRIED UNITED STATES AND CALIFORNIA, 1920-1970

Table 1

WOMEN'S AGE AT MARRIAGE: CALIFORNIA, 1966-1971; UNITED STATES, 1962-1971

Year	Median age at marriage		First quartile age at marriage		Interquartile range (Q_3 - Q_1)	
	California	U.S.	California	U.S.	California	U.S.
1971	20.8	20.9	19.0	19.0	4.3	4.5
1970	20.7	20.8	18.9	18.9	4.1	4.4
1969	20.6	20.8	18.8	18.9	3.9	4.3
1968	20.5	20.8	18.8	18.9	3.8	4.4
1967	20.3	20.6	18.8	18.8	3.8	4.0
1966	20.2	20.5	18.7	18.7	3.9	4.1
1965	n.a.	20.6	n.a.	18.7	n.a.	4.0
1964	n.a.	20.5	n.a.	18.7	n.a.	3.7
1963	n.a.	20.5	n.a.	18.6	n.a.	3.9
1962	n.a.	20.3	n.a.	18.4	n.a.	3.8
1961	n.a.	20.3	n.a.	n.a.	n.a.	n.a.
1960	19.9	20.3	18.3	n.a.	4.2	n.a.

Sources: For U.S. data, U.S. Bureau of Census (1971b); for California data, California Department of Public Health (1971), and unpublished data.

RECORD LINKAGE

In linking records, the task of the investigator is to search the information on one type of record (such as a marriage certificate) to see if it agrees with or matches identifying information on another record (such as a birth record). If the records clearly seem to refer to the same person or persons, then the records are "linked" and a family history has begun to be built. Conceptually, the problem is simple. The technique is simple also if a small number of records is to be matched and an extensive amount of identifying information is common to the different records (such as name, address, age, birthplace, occupation, etc.). Linking vital records for California was technically more complex. The number of records was very large and the amount of identifying information was sufficient, but not extensive. These complexities required computerizing the record linkage process.

Until recently, most record linkages of marriage and birth records have been done manually. Records were visually inspected, sorted by hand, and decisions were based on the judgment of the investigator about the quality of each match. There are, obviously, physical human limits to the number of records that can be processed manually. Large files of records, such as those in California where in one year, 1966, there were more than 100,000 women married for the first time, require computerization of the matching procedure if record linkage is to be a feasible means of generating data.

Computerized linkages of records from diverse sources pertaining to the same individuals were developed in the early 1960s, in Canada by Newcombe [1965a]. Newcombe's matching system was based principally on a systematic programming of the kinds of decisions a human clerk makes when records are matched by hand. His success in computerized linkages of records, and a growing recognition of the usefulness of record linkage, sparked a brief flurry of analyses in the late sixties of the theoretical bases of the decision-making process involved in matching records. Mathematical models of the record linkage procedure were developed by DuBois [1969], Fellegi and Sunter [1969] and Tepping [1968]. Of these theories, the most general and widely applicable is that put forth by Fellegi and Sunter. The data for this study were generated by a modification of the Fellegi and Sunter techniques.

Although complicated in its detail, the logic of the record linkage procedure remains simple. If the researcher picks up a marriage record, then the birth records must be searched to find any and all children born to that couple. A similar procedure is required for linking divorces and infant deaths. However, since the California Department of Public Health had already linked births to infant deaths, it was not necessary to repeat that record linkage for this study. The reader is referred to Appendix A for a more technical discussion of the record linkage procedure.

In linking vital records for this study, the major problems were (a) the omission of California residents who married out of state, and (b) loss of women from the record linkage framework with the passage of time after marriage. Figure 2 illustrates the way in which a woman's marriage and the subsequent events of childbirth or divorce might or might not get matched. Out-of-state marriages occurred particularly in Nevada. According to the Nevada State Health Department, approximately 45,000 California residents of all ages were married in Nevada in 1966.[1] This number represents 24 percent of the California residents married in either California or Nevada in that year. It is also possible that some of the people who married in California in 1966 did so without intending to live in California. However, it is likely that their number is insignificantly small.

Those couples married out-of-state never enter into the record linkage framework, and it is somewhat difficult to assess what bias might be introduced by their omission, especially since we are not even sure of their ages. The difficulty arises because Nevada, the most popular locale for Californians' out-of-state marriages, asks for no identifying information of couples marrying in the state except for their addresses and names. In Washoe County, which encompasses the Reno-Sparks area, even the question of residence is typically omitted from the marriage certificate. What little information we do have

---

[1] Estimates obtained through personal communication with John Sullivan, Chief, Bureau of Vital Statistics, Nevada State Health Department. This figure includes all marriages, not just first marriages. No data were available on the number of previous marriages of the bride and groom.

comes from the California divorce records, themselves a potentially biased source of information. These records, on which place of marriage is recorded, are discussed in greater detail in Weeks [1972]. The indication is that Nevada marriages tend to underrepresent first marriages. Associated with that is the fact that California residents married in Nevada tend to be older on the average than those married in California. Although spur-of-the-moment elopements romantically are associated

Figure 2

California Residents Who Married in 1966
Classified by Their Potential Status with
Respect to the Record-Linkage Framework

All California Residents Who Married in 1966							
Married in California				Married Out-of-State			
No Out-of-State Move During First Year of Marriage		Did Move		No Move		Did Move	
Vital Event During 1st Yr. of Mar. *	No Vital Event	Vital Event	No Vital Event	Vital Event	No Vital Event	Vital Event	No Vital Event
		Before Move / After Move					
Match / No Match		Match / No Match					

*The term vital event means birth of a child or a divorce complaint.

with the young, there is a tendency for older persons, and persons who have been to the altar previously, to take greater advantage of Nevada's marriage laws than do young couples. Thus, teenagers are less likely to be married in Nevada than older couples.

The advantage of marrying in Nevada, it might be noted, is that since Nevada does not require a test for venereal disease prior to marriage (although it is against the law in Nevada to marry if you are so afflicted) and since marriage licenses may be obtained and services performed virtually any time of the day or night in most areas of that state, a couple can marry at a moment's notice. In California, by contrast, the venereal disease test and the more normal business hours of the county clerks means that at least three days usually elapse between the decision to marry and the fact of marriage. Furthermore, the nightclubs and casinos in Reno and Las Vegas provide attractive entertainment for a wedding party. However, such activity would not be available to teenage couples.

A more significant problem arises in determining which couples moved out of California after marriage, and when they moved. It is unreasonable to presume that all women remained within the state even during the limited time period under investigation (1966-1969). Some women moved after giving birth to a child, some before a birth. Some moved after obtaining a divorce, some before divorcing. Some moved without any vital event other than marriage occurring to them in California. Estimating the extent to which couples tended to leave the state and thereby exited from the linkage framework was an integral step in deriving the appropriate numbers of women at risk of the vital events that were matched. The reader is referred to Appendix B for a detailed account of how those numbers were derived.

Overall, the linkage of vital records provided information about teenage marriages which might otherwise not have been available. Data were required on the behavior of a highly specifiable population (teenagers marrying for the first time), but the information desired was somewhat sensitive (births, infant deaths, divorces), and possibly prone to error if the information had not been elicited carefully in a well-constructed interview. Furthermore, surveying this many persons would have been an incredibly expensive task. Of course, a sample could have been drawn, but it too would have been extremely costly, as well as time consuming, in comparison to the use of the records alone. Record linkage thus provided a quick, convenient, and relatively economical means to obtain potentially sensitive information.

2
THE TREND IN
TEENAGE MARRIAGES

Teenage marriages as used in the context of this book are those in which the bride has not yet reached her twentieth birthday. In succeeding chapters, it will be noted that the age of the groom also has important implications for the history of a marriage, but the age of the bride is of greater demographic concern since she is the childbearer.

RECENT TRENDS IN THE UNITED STATES

According to the 1970 census, 11.9 percent of all women aged 15-19 were married. Historically, this is a fairly low proportion. As Table 2 shows, for all races the proportion married rose steadily between 1900 and 1930. Over the long run, the economic prosperity that has accompanied the processes of industrialization and urbanization has made it increasingly easier for couples (and especially men) to marry young because it has become easier to obtain either a stable well-paying job or to find familial or governmental assistance for a young family [see, for example, Easterlin, 1968]. Marriage among teenagers increased slightly from the turn of the century to the Depression, leveled off during that dismal period, then rose dramatically during the economic expansion following World War II. The recent decline in the proportion of teenagers married seems to be related to the inflation of the 1960s and 1970s and the recession of the 1970s.

Table 2
PERCENT OF TEENAGERS EVER-MARRIED:
UNITED STATES, 1900-1970

| Year | Percent ever-married, aged 15-19 | | | | | |
| | All races | | White | | Nonwhite | |
	Male	Female	Male	Female	Male	Female
1900	1.0	11.3	0.9	10.4	1.9	17.0
1910	1.2	11.7	1.0	10.7	2.3	18.4
1920	2.1	12.9	1.9	11.8	4.0	21.2
1930	1.8	13.1	1.5	11.8	3.6	21.9
1940	1.7	11.9	1.6	10.9	3.2	19.0
1950	3.3	17.1	3.2	16.5	4.4	21.1
1960	3.9	16.1	3.9	16.1	3.8	16.2
1970	4.1	11.9	4.1	12.0	4.5	11.3

Source: Sklar and Berkov, 1974:82.

Table 2 also shows that racial differences in teenage marriages have been in evidence throughout this century. Nonwhites had significantly higher proportions of teenage women married than whites from 1900 to 1940. During that period of time the proportions for nonwhites rose slightly from 1900 to 1930 and then declined slightly during the Depression, a pattern similar to that for whites. However, the early post-World War II prosperity did not affect the proportion of nonwhite teenage women who were married nearly as much as it affected white women. Between 1940 and 1950 there was a 51 percent increase in the proportion of white teenage women who were married, but only an 11 percent increase for nonwhites. However, since 1950 the proportion of teenage women married has declined more for nonwhites than for whites. Sklar and Berkov [1974a:85] and Farley [1970:141] have also noted these racial differences in teenage marital patterns.

The swing of economic events is generally consistent with the swing of other events relating to the proportion of teenagers who are married. An even closer fit exists, however, when we compare changes in the proportion of teenagers married with the *rate of expansion* of the economy. In other words, the proportion of teenagers married varies less with the actual level of economic prosperity than it does with the rate at which the economy is expanding. Thus, the fact that during the 1940s the economy expanded at a more rapid rate than ever before in recorded American history is related to the rapid increases in the proportion of teenagers married. The slight decline in the proportion of teenagers married during the fifties is related to the fact that during this time, although the economy was expanding, the rate was lower than during the forties. During the 1960s the economy continued in a growth recession—an expansion at ever-declining rates— and the proportion of teenagers marrying continued to drop off. These data are presented in Table 3.

Economic factors may also help explain the racial differences in teenage marital patterns. The variations in teenage marriages for both white and nonwhite populations clearly are in line with economic fluctuations. The principal underlying racial differential is that before 1960, nonwhite teenage women exhibited a much greater tendency to be married than did their white counterparts. This may well be due to the more heavily rural nature of the black population until after World War II. Farley [1970:50] has noted that the urbanization of the black population in this country has lagged about thirty years behind the rest of the population. Since World War II the social and economic differences between whites and non-whites have narrowed considerably. Thus it is not surprising to find the demographic phenomena recently becoming more standardized racially.

Table 3
TEENAGE MARRIAGES AND ECONOMIC GROWTH: UNITED STATES, 1910-1970 (IN PERCENT)

| | | Per decade change in: | |
Year	Ever-married women 15-19	Proportion of teenage women married	Gross National Product (constant dollars)
1910	11.7		
1920	12.9	+10.3	+23.6
1930	13.1	+ 1.6	+32.4
1940	11.9	- 9.2	+10.1
1950	17.1	+43.7	+58.5
1960	16.1	- 0.1	+40.5
1970	11.9	-26.1	+31.9

Source: Sklar and Berkov, 1974:82; Easterlin, 1968:208-209; United Nations, 1973b:536.

The most notable recent change in the incidence of teenage marriages, regardless of race, is clearly the sharp decline during the 1960s. We might well ask whether this phenomenon was "real" or a demographic artifact. For example, changes in the distribution of teenagers by single years of age could have influenced the proportion of the total who were married. The changing size of birth cohorts during the baby boom could have affected the distribution of women.

Indeed, there was a slight shift in the distribution of teenagers in the 15-19 group between 1960 and 1970. However, the direction of the changes would have suggested a smaller dip than actually occurred in the proportion of teenagers married. The most marriageable teen years—ages 18 and 19—rose from 37 percent of all those 15-19 years old in 1960 to 39 percent in 1970. As Table 4 shows, the declines in the incidence of marriage were shared quite equally by each single

Table 4
TEENAGE MARRIAGES BY SINGLE YEAR OF AGE: UNITED STATES 1960-1970 (IN PERCENT)

Age	Ever-married		Change
	1960	1970	1960-1970
15	2.4	1.8	-25
16	5.7	3.9	-32
17	12.1	8.5	-30
18	24.5	17.5	-29
19	40.4	29.5	-27
15-19	16.1	11.9	-26

Source: U.S. Bureau of the Census, 1963: Table 1; 1973: Table 1.

year of age in the 15-19 year age group. Between 1960 and 1970, the declines in the proportion of teenagers married were obviously occasioned by "real" declines in the marriage rates. The consequence was to lower the overall fertility of the teenage population as well. To look at more recent changes in marriage rates and teenage fertility, we can examine data from California.

MARRIAGE RATES IN CALIFORNIA

   Sklar and Berkov [1974a:84] have estimated the first-
marriage rates for females in California for every year between 1960 and 1972. Between 1960 and 1965 there was an
uninterrupted decline in the marriage rate for all women,
but especially for teenagers. The years 1966 to 1968 saw a
slight upturn in marriage rates, coinciding with the rise in
the draft call for the Vietnam war. During this period of
time, marriage—especially marriage with parenthood—
provided young males with a hedge against the draft. From
1969 to 1971 the marriage rates resumed their downward
trend. The slight rise in 1972 possibly reflected the return
home of young Vietnam veterans ready to get married and
settle down.
   By telescoping Sklar and Berkov's data slightly, an interesting phenomenon can be observed. Figure 3 shows that marriage
rates between 1960 and 1965 dropped 20 percent for women
aged 15-19 but only 4 percent for women aged 20-24. Between 1965 and 1970, marriage rates for teenagers dropped
8 percent, but rates for women aged 20-24 dropped by 14
percent. The women who were 15-19 in 1960-1965 were the
same women who were 20-24 in 1965-1970. These women,
born during the 1940s, the initial products of the baby boom,
apparently led the movement toward declining rates of
marriage. Analysis of single-year-of-age data revealed that one
birth cohort, that of 1947, in fact accounted for almost all
of the change. In every year, their marriage rates were tend-
ing to go up slightly at the older ages while they were going
down among younger women, a tendency that also suggests a
noneconomic influence, the marriage squeeze.
   The marriage squeeze is a demographic situation in which
there are too many women of marriageable age relative to the
number of men a few years senior in age who are the typically
sought-after marriage partners [see, e.g., Muhsam, 1974]. The

condition is created by the inequality in size of successive birth cohorts. From 1945-1957 each birth cohort was larger than the one of the previous year, and so women born during this period faced stiff competition for men who were older

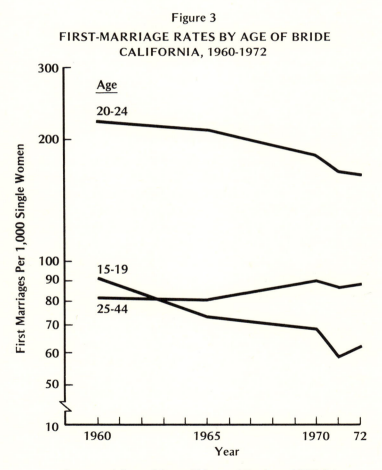

Figure 3

**FIRST-MARRIAGE RATES BY AGE OF BRIDE
CALIFORNIA, 1960-1972**

Source: Adapted from Sklar and Berkov, 1974:84.

than themselves. One solution, of course, was to wait for men of more nearly the same age. Since men typically marry at a slightly older age than women, the consequence was a rise in the age at marriage for women. Since the birth cohorts have been successively smaller since 1957, the marriage squeeze for women should abate in the late 1970s.

For men, the marriage squeeze has speeded up the long and dramatic decline in the age at marriage among males. Between 1950 and 1970, as the percentage of teenage women who were married declined, the proportion of teenage males who were married increased.

VARIATIONS WITHIN THE TEEN YEARS

The marriage squeeze helps to explain some of the variation in marriage rates in a broad way. Certainly within the teen years, however, the variations suggest that other factors were also operating. For example the slight rise in the marriage rates for women aged 15-19 between 1967-1969 was accounted for entirely by women aged 15-17 (see Figure 4). From 1966 to 1971 the marriage rates for 18-19 year old women declined without interruption.

Between 1970 and 1971 there was a steep drop in the marriage rate for 15-17 year old women. The availability of legal abortions apparently resulted in greater numbers of premarital pregnancies increasing abortion use rather than instigating marriages. However, the 18-19 year olds seemed unaffected by the abortion law. As noted earlier, the marriage rates for 15-18 year olds rebounded slightly in 1972, concomitant with the 1971 to 1972 deescalation of the Vietnam war. Futhermore, there was considerable national debate about abortion, and strong anti-abortion feeling was generated. This perhaps helped to make some young women, especially younger teenagers, reluctant to seek and doctors reluctant to per-

form an abortion they might have chosen willingly the year
before. In 1972, the California State Supreme Court struck
down a restrictive clause in the law that had forced women
to develop elaborate reasons for wanting an abortion. With

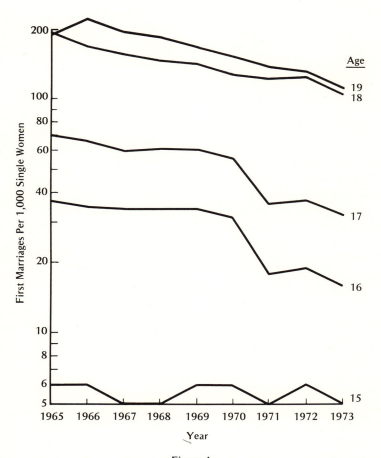

Figure 4
TEENAGE FIRST MARRIAGE RATES, CALIFORNIA, 1965-1973

that restriction removed in November of 1972, from 1972 to 1973 the marriage rates declined for all of the teen years to a point below the 1971 levels.

Throughout this discussion, I have implied that changes in the use of abortion as an anti-birth measure will lower marriage rates by providing an alternative to marriage as a response to a premarital pregnancy. Although not fully substantiated, the implication is reasonable, for among younger teenagers a higher proportion of marriages are associated with pregnancies than among older teenagers. Therefore, marriage rates among 15-17 year olds will be more responsive to changes in abortion utilization than marriage rates among 18-19 year olds.

Over time, then, the proportion of teenagers married has fluctuated in tandem with social and economic changes, as have changes in the birth rate and in childlessness as well. The next chapter examines the relationship between teenage marriages and fertility.

3

TEENAGE MARRIAGES AND FERTILITY

Characteristically, teenage brides become teenage mothers, and quickly. According to data from the 1964-1966 National Natality Survey, 70 percent of all married first-time mothers age 15-19 had borne their first child during the first year of marriage [National Center for Health Statistics, 1970a]. By contrast, among women who were 20-24 when their first child was born, only half as many—35 percent—had born their child during the first twelve months of marriage. The percentages declined steadily with older cohorts: to 17 among women aged 25-29, to 15 for those aged 30-34, and to 13 percent among women aged 35-44.

Sklar and Berkov [1974a:82] note that women married at ages under 23 have recently reversed the tendency toward earlier childbearing within marriage. However, Current Population Surveys indicate that this does not pertain to women married between the ages of 14-18. Their tendency to bear children early in marriage continued unabated through 1965-1969, the most recent period for which data are available. It can be seen in Table 5 that among women aged 14-18 when they married in 1960-1964, 43.3 percent had borne a first child within twelve months after marriage, and 64.8 percent within eighteen months after marriage. Among women

of that same age marrying in 1965-1969, 44.0 percent had
borne a child within twelve months after marriage and 65.2
percent within eighteen months. It should be noted, though,
that the increase is generally accounted for by the increases
over time in the number of brides who have borne an illegitimate child prior to marriage.

Table 5

TIMING OF FIRST BIRTH EARLY IN MARRIAGE
AMONG WHITE WOMEN WHO MARRIED BETWEEN AGES OF 14-18:
UNITED STATES, 1930-1969
(IN PERCENT)

Year of first marriage	Months of marriage until first birth	
	12	18
1930-1939	29.5	58.0
1940-1949	28.2	56.2
1950-1959	38.8	64.9
1960-1964	43.3	64.8
1965-1969	44.0	65.2

Source: U.S. Bureau of Census, *Current Population Reports,* "Fertility Histories
and Birth Expectations of American Women: June, 1971," Series P-20, #263,
April 1974, Table 18.

In this same vein we can note that as the age at marriage
declined in this country, the average age of mothers at childbirth, regardless of their total number of children (their
parity), also declined [National Center for Health Statistics,
1968]. In essence, the intervals between marriage and births
have either remained constant or declined [Glick and Parke,
1965]. In 1966, for example, the median age of mothers at
the birth of the second (i.e., generational replacing) child was
only 24.2, down from 25.6 in 1940. It is of interest to note
that a decrease in the number of years between generations
can alone raise the growth rate of the population.

COMPLETED FAMILY SIZE AMONG TEENAGE BRIDES

It is obvious that early ages at marriage imply longer periods of time during which a woman is exposed to the risk of child-bearing. Of course, risks are not necessarily converted into actual behavior. In a "natural" population using no birth preventive measures, we would expect to find that the young-er a woman is when she marries, the more children she will have borne when she completes her reproductive career. Few, if any, populations have ever been truly natural, and so the relationship between age at marriage and completed fertility is not empirically close. Campbell has recently argued that "regardless of how much earlier child-bearing may be asso-ciated with higher completed fertility in cross-sectional studies, they are not necessarily associated in time series or in inter-national comparisons" [Campbell, 1974:556].

Although the relationship is a bit cloudy, the fact that on an a priori basis we expect a strong negative relationship between age at marriage and completed family size means that any apparent departures from that pattern warrant attention. Indeed, even with the currently most sophisticated contracep-tive technology, the chance for preventive failure exists. The longer a population is exposed to the risk of contraceptive failure, the higher its fertility is likely to be. No population has ever been sufficiently motivated to test the effectiveness of contraceptives (or abortions) to the limit of their potential. Thus, we find that, according to the United States Census of 1960, among women who had completed their childbearing, those who had married between the ages of 14-17 had borne nearly twice as many children as those who married at ages 30-44. In fact, on average, women married at ages 14-17 had one more child even than women first married between the ages of 20-21 [U.S. Bureau of Census, 1960]. This same rela-tionship held up in the 1970 census. In Table 6 it can be seen that for each successive birth cohort, women married at ages

14-17 were bearing at least 8 percent more children than women married at ages 18-19. In turn this latter group of women had at least 11 percent more children than women married at ages 22-24.

Table 6

AGE AT FIRST MARRIAGE AND CHILDREN EVER BORN: U.S. WHITE WOMEN, 1970 (IN PERCENT)

	Age in 1970						
	20-24	25-29	30-34	35-39	40-44	45-49	50+
By 1970, women married at age 14-17 had borne more children than women married at age 18-19 by:	69	25	14	9	8	13	17
By 1970, women married at age 18-19 had borne more children than women married at age 22-24 by:	116[a]	94	31	17	11	11	29

[a] Data for age 22-24 not available; 20-24 used instead.
Source: U.S. Bureau of Census, 1970 Census of Population, Subject Reports, Women by Number of Children Ever Born, P-107.

TEENAGE FERTILITY AND ABORTION IN CALIFORNIA

Abortions have been legal in California since 1967, but only since 1970 has there been any apparently substantial public awareness of their legality for pregnant teenagers. Futhermore, in that year hospitals tended to be more permissive with respect to allowing abortions. As a result, of the 84,000 abortions performed between November 1967, when the Therapeutic Abortion Law became effective, and the end of 1970, 75 percent were performed in 1970 [Jackson, 1971:229].

Even after 1970 the impact of abortions on teenage fertility was not dramatic. Before that, as Table 7 shows, the birth rates for teenagers rose between 1940 and 1960, then declined

Table 7
AGE-SPECIFIC BIRTH RATES FOR CALIFORNIA AND THE U.S.:
1940-1970

Live births per 1,000 women in:	Age of mother					
	15-19	20-24	25-29	30-34	35-39	40-44
1940						
California	48	134	109	65	29	8
United States	54	136	123	83	46	16
1950						
California	92	204	159	93	43	11
United States	82	197	166	104	53	15
1960						
California	103	264	189	103	48	12
United States	89	258	197	112	56	15
1970						
California	69	158	106		18	
United States	68	168	145	73	32	8

Source: 1940-1960 data from NCHS (1967); 1970 data for U.S. from NCHS (1974); 1970 data for California from Berkov and Sklar (1972).

substantially in California and in the whole United States between 1960 and 1970. Within the teen years, Figure 5 illustrates that age-specific birth rates showed declines between 1960 and 1970 for all ages except for age 15. However, in the late 1960s birth rates for 15-17 year old women had either leveled off or were rising slightly. Between 1970 and 1971, virtually identical declines in birth rates were registered by each age from 15 through 19 apparently as a consequence of a rise in abortions. The 1972 California State Supreme Court

decision, which further liberalized the abortion law in California, apparently provided a stimulus for a decline in the
birth rate among 15-17 year old women, but this was small,
and the liberalization had no appreciable effect overall for
18-19 year olds.

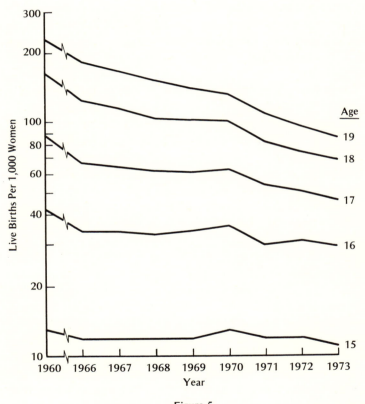

Figure 5
TEENAGE FERTILITY RATES, CALIFORNIA, 1960-1973

Teenage fertility is especially influenced by the combination of legitimate and illegitimate fertility, here including as legitimate all births following upon marriage regardless of the time interval elapsed. In Figure 6, I have estimated fertility rates broken down accordingly. With the exception of age 15, it can be said that in 1973, the lower the age, the higher the level of legitimate childbearing. This could be expected. As we shall see in Chapter 4, the younger the age at marriage, the greater is the likelihood that the bride was pregnant. That fact alone could account for the differences in legitimate fertility rates by age. Illegitimate fertility rates exhibit the opposite pattern—the higher the age, the higher the illegitimate fertility rates.

We cannot place too much stock in these rates because they do not reflect accurately the population at risk. It is usual practice to assume that women at risk of giving birth to an illegitimate child are all single. This assumes that all single women are sexually active, which is not the case for young teenagers [Kantner and Zelnick, 1972b]. Since among teenagers more of the older are sexually active than the younger, the total number of single women more accurately reflects the older than the younger teenage women at risk of an illegitimate birth.

To avoid the problem of inaccuracy in the base population, we can analyze the differences in legitimate and illegitimate births by looking at the illegitimacy ratio—the proportion of all births that are illegitimate. Between 1966 and 1973 there was a changing mix of legitimate and illegitimate births to teenagers of all ages. As can be seen in Figure 7, the older the teenager, the more rapid has been the recent rise in the proportion of all births that are illegitimate. Note, too, the interruption in that rise during the 1970-1971 period when abortions were apparently "discovered" in California. Such changes explain, for example, the facts that (a) in Figure 5, teenage fertility rates for women age 17 show a decline between 1966

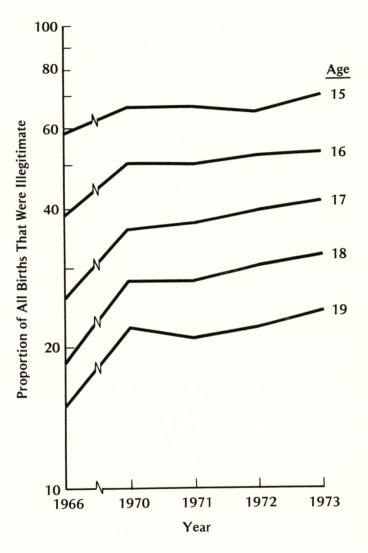

Figure 6
**PROPORTION OF ALL TEENAGE BIRTHS
THAT WERE ILLEGITIMATE, CALIFORNIA, 1966-1973**

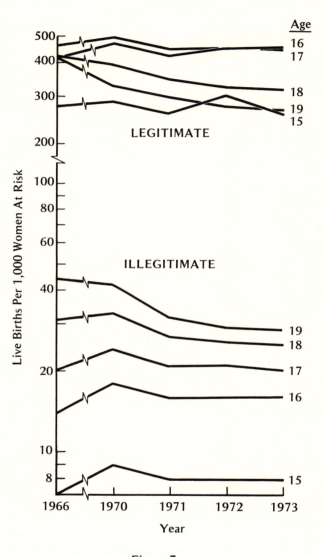

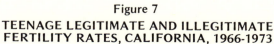

Figure 7
**TEENAGE LEGITIMATE AND ILLEGITIMATE
FERTILITY RATES, CALIFORNIA, 1966-1973**

and 1970, yet (b) in Figure 7, both legitimate and illegitimate fertility rates for 17 year old women went up during that period. Declining proportions of women married, coupled with an increasing tendency for those births that occurred to be illegitimate, meant that the influence of legitimate fertility on overall teenage fertility declined during this period, even though the legitimate fertility rate was rising.

Also of interest in Figure 7 is the continued differentiation in behavior between the 15-17 and the 18-19 year old women. Although the abortion "revolution" of 1970-1971 hit all ages 15-19 about equally, up until that time marital fertility had been increasing among the younger but decreasing among the older cadres. Furthermore, 15-17 year olds seemed to be much more influenced by anti-abortion feeling during the 1971-1972 period than were 18-19 year olds. Even illegitimate fertility had been declining among 19-year-old women from 1966-1970, while it had been increasing for younger women.

Perhaps the most significant aspect of these data on single years of age is that they help to explain, at least statistically, why teenage illegitimacy was rising in the late 1960s while marital birthrates were apparently declining.

In general, the data in Figures 5 through 7 indicate that different things were happening at different ages. Among 15-17 year old women, both marital and nonmarital fertility rates rose during the late 1960s. Concomitantly, among 19 year olds both rates fell. Only among 18 year olds did marital fertility fall while nonmarital fertility rates rose. At almost all ages the 1971-1973 data indicate a leveling off of the 1970-1971 fertility declines. However, the January 1973 United States Supreme Court ruling allowing abortions to be performed in doctors' offices and clinics as well as in hospitals may well be having the effect of making abortions more attractive to teenagers as well as to older women. It will probably also have the effect in California of lowering the number of reported abortions. Doctors are not currently required to report abortions done outside of hospitals.

ILLEGITIMATE CONCEPTIONS AND TEENAGE MARRIAGE

In California between 1970 and 1971, rates for both illegitimacy and marriage for teenage women dropped. This suggests that some teenage marriages are forced by the discovery of a pregnancy. If the pregnancy is terminated, the marriage need not take place. In the same vein, an increase in the illegitimate birth rate for teenage women in California between 1971 and 1972 tended to be accompanied by a rise in the marriage rate for teenage women.

Although illegitimacy and teenage marriage are related to each other, there is not necessarily a one-to-one congruence. As can be seen by comparing Figures 4 and 7, while marriage rates for teenagers declined during the 1960s, illegitimate birth rates continued to rise.

Apparently, then, the relationship between illegitimacy and teenage marriage is two-edged. Over the long run, a given set of circumstances can produce contrasting trends in these two phenomena. In the short run, however, even with abortions and contraceptives available to teenagers, a certain proportion of teenage marriages are still brought on by the discovery of an illegitimate pregnancy. It is to this topic that we turn next.

4

PREMARITAL PREGNANCIES AND EARLY MARRIAGE

Teenagers are much more likely than older women to be pregnant when they marry. This is true partly because of high rates of illegitimate conceptions among teenagers, and also because a nonmarried pregnant teenager is more likely to get married than an older nonmarried pregnant woman. As is true with marriage and fertility rates, there are significant behavioral differences even within the teen years with respect to the incidence of premarital pregnancies. In general, the younger the bride, the higher the probability that she will be pregnant. This relationship depends on other factors, however, such as the characteristics of the groom, race, and ethnicity. In this chapter, these demographic aspects of teenage premarital pregnancies are analyzed, drawing heavily upon data from the 1966 marriage cohort in California.

PREMARITAL PREGNANCIES AND AGE AT MARRIAGE

To say that teenagers are more prone toward premarital pregnancies than older women could easily be an understatement. Table 8 and Figure 8 show the premarital pregnancy rates for women married in California in 1966. Women of that specific group who bore a child within six and a half months of marriage are what I call "early premarital conceivers" and those who bore a child between six-and-a-half and eight months after marriage are "late premarital conceivers." Among 15 year old brides, 45 percent bore a child within six and a half months, and 59 percent within eight months after marriage. But the percentage drops quickly by age. For example, among 19 year old brides, 18 percent bore a child

Table 8

PREMARITAL PREGNANCIES BY AGE AT FIRST MARRIAGE: CALIFORNIA MARRIAGE COHORT, 1966 (IN PERCENT)

Age at first marriage	Birth within months of marriage:			Percentage within 6½ months
	6½	6½-8	8	
15	45.1	13.9	59.0	76
16	30.3	13.1	43.4	70
17	25.4	11.8	37.2	68
18	15.3	8.1	23.4	65
19	11.4	6.6	18.0	63
20	9.0	5.1	14.1	64
21	6.4	4.6	11.0	58
22-24	5.3	3.4	8.7	61
25-29	4.5	2.9	7.4	61
30-34	3.6	2.3	5.9	61
35-44	1.8	1.1	2.9	62
TOTAL	11.7	6.2	17.9	65
χ^2	167.0	31.9	198.9	
N(Women at Risk)b	102,230	99,383	*a	

aRepresents a summation of data for 6½ months and 6½-8 months—not calculated independently.

bData are adjusted for migration.

during the first eight months of marriage. That figure is 41 percentage points less than for the 15 year olds, but only 15 percentage points more than for women aged 35-44 at marriage! The biggest change among teenagers, in terms of the

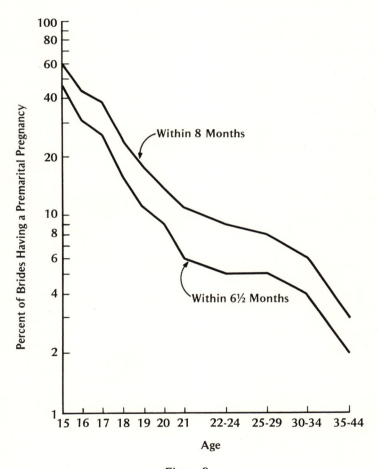

Figure 8
PREMARITAL PREGNANCIES BY AGE
AT FIRST MARRIAGE, CALIFORNIA, 1966

percentage change between adjacent age groups, comes between the 17 and the 18 year old brides. Between these two
close age groups occurs the largest percentage decline in the
proportion of pregnant brides. Differences between these age
groups have already been discussed in Chapter 3 with respect
to both legitimate and illegitimate fertility. It is probably
significant that this age break also represents the difference
between a girl who is likely to have graduated from high school
and one who has not.

In American culture, marriage and childbearing before high
school is completed have been normatively proscribed during
the past few decades. It was not unusual during the 1960s to
find married, and especially pregnant, girls set apart in special
curricula in the high schools. This generally reflects the closer
adult supervision over the behavior of persons under age 18
than over those ages 18 and older. Thus, the social pressures
brought to bear on a younger teenager to postpone marriage
are undoubtedly greater than on an older teenager.

Young teenagers also tend to marry later in relation to the
timing of pregnancy than do older women. This is evidenced
by the findings, shown in the last column of Table 8, that
three-fourths of all pregnant brides age 15 bore their child
within six and a half months after marriage compared to two-
thirds of women age 18, and slightly less than two-thirds of
older women. The data suggest that, as might be expected,
the younger the girl, the more likely it is that marriage follows the discovery of pregnancy, rather than vice versa. This
relationship is also evidenced by data on the incidence of
births within the first three months of marriage. Among girls
married at age 15, 11 percent had a child within three months
after marriage. At age 16, the percentage declines to 6, then
down to 4 at age 17, 3 at age 18, 2 at age 19, and 1 percent
or less at all older ages.

In Table 8 and several subsequent tables I have employed
chi-square as a goodness-of-fit test. It is a measure of the ex-

tent to which, in this example, the percentage of women bearing a child during a given interval after marriage was the same for every age. I have employed the percentage for all ages 15-44 as the expected value. It can be seen in Table 8 that there is considerably more variation by age during the first six and a half months of marriage (χ^2 = 167.0) than during the period from six and a half to eight months (χ^2 = 31.9). The chi-square values thus provide an index of the steepness of the age-gradient in the timing of the first birth. To add to this methodological aside, it should be noted that the term "premarital pregnancy rates" will be used interchangeably with the term "proportion of brides who were pregnant." This is done largely for purposes of shorthand, but the two terms statistically are very close to one another. A rate expresses the frequency with which an event occurs in relation to some fixed unit of measurement. The proportion of brides who are pregnant can be interpreted as the frequency per 100 brides with which pregnancy is present at marriage.

In the literature reporting data by single years of age within the teen years, I have found only two previous studies. One of these [Lowrie, 1965] showed a steep gradient in the decline of premarital pregnancies by age within the teenages, whereas the other [Monahan, 1960], did not. It is significant, however, that Lowrie's study was a linkage of births to all marriages occurring in a county in Ohio between 1957 and 1962, whereas Monahan's data were drawn quite selectively from among people who were seeking help for a troubled marriage.

In Lowrie's study, 33 percent of the brides aged 16 or less bore a child within six and a half months after marriage, with the percentages going down to 23 for age 17, to 12 for age 18, and down further to only 6 percent for brides aged 19. Thus, Lowrie's data show a decline of 27 percentage points between age 19 and the oldest age group, 25 and older.

Data generated for the three studies all show a clear tendency

for premarital pregnancies to decline as age increases. Those
for the present study show the steepest decline, followed by
Lowrie's, then by Monahan's. These differences could be due
to the differences in the methods employed to obtain the data.
They may also be due, at least in part, to the time sequence of
events. Monahan's data refer to 1954, Lowrie's to 1957-1962,
and mine to 1966. It is quite possible that over time, older
teenagers and young adult women have become (1) relatively
more efficient in avoiding pregnancy than younger teenagers
(a possibility consistent with recent trends in illegitimacy rates),
and (2) relatively less inclined to marry when illegitimately
pregnant than younger teenagers.

PREMARITAL PREGNANCY AND THE GROOM'S CHARACTERISTICS

On a priori grounds, it might be expected that previously
married men would be more likely than never previously married men to initiate early sexual activity with a girl. Being
more accustomed to regular sexual activity, and perhaps being
more experienced sexually, previously married men might be
expected to initiate more premarital pregnancies than never-
married men. On the other hand, it is within marriage, especially
of younger people, that the greatest knowledge about contraceptives is acquired [see, e.g., Rainwater, 1965:212]. Thus, a
man who has been married before should be expected to know
more about contraceptives and possibly be more likely therefore to use them or to instruct his partner in their use if premarital sexual activity occurs.

The data for California suggest that among teenage brides,
marrying a previously married man reduces the likelihood of
pregnancy at marriage. This excludes the 15 year olds, for
whom the number of cases is too small to be of much significance (see Table 9). Above age 19, however, the differences
in rates of premarital pregnancy vary little with the groom's

marital history, and there is no consistent pattern, either, except for a general decline by age.

Two conclusions can be drawn from Table 9: (1) as the age of never-before-married brides increases, more of their bridegrooms have been married previously; (2) previously married bridegrooms appear less likely than never-married men to be marrying a pregnant teenager. This latter point could be due to differences in premarital sexual activity, but more likely it is due to more effective contraceptive use among men married before. It is also possible that a previously married man is more likely to break off relations with a girl who becomes pregnant than to marry her. It is also likely, especially for a teenage woman, that a previously married man will also be

Table 9

PREMARITAL PREGNANCIES ACCORDING TO GROOM'S MARITAL HISTORY, BY AGE OF BRIDE AT MARRIAGE, AND PERCENTAGE OF BRIDES MARRYING A PREVIOUSLY MARRIED MAN: CALIFORNIA MARRIAGE COHORT, 1966 (IN PERCENT)

Age of bride	First birth within months of marriage				Brides of previously married men
	0 - 6½		6½ - 8		
	Previously married:				
	No	Yes	No	Yes	
15	45.0	50.0	12.5	20.0	1.0
16	30.2	20.9	12.8	4.5	2.2
17	25.2	20.0	11.5	4.6	2.9
18	14.9	12.7	7.8	4.0	4.2
19	11.1	10.1	6.3	4.0	5.6
20	8.6	9.5	4.8	3.9	7.3
21	5.9	8.8	4.3	4.0	9.0
22-24	5.0	5.9	3.2	3.1	14.1
25-29	4.4	4.2	2.9	2.4	25.0
30-34	3.6	3.1	2.4	1.8	36.2
35-44	2.2	1.3	1.0	1.3	48.7

older than she. As we shall see, the age of the husband affects the likelihood of a premarital pregnancy.

Since very few teenage women, especially young teenagers, marry men younger than, or even the same age as, themselves, the entire group of teenagers, from ages 15-19, was coalesced for this part of the analysis. It appears that among teenage brides in California the incidence of a premaritally conceived birth is related to the relative age of the groom (see Table 10). If the groom is younger, the chance of conception is highest. If the groom is older, the chance of conception is least. These data are quite probably explicable in terms of the knowledge of, and use of, contraceptives on the part of older men. Virtually all of the difference in birth timing by relative age of husband is attributable to premarital conception, suggesting that after marriage, equity is achieved in contraceptive usage among all couples, regardless of the groom's relative age.

If we examine a group of older brides—for example, those aged 25—we might well expect to find the difference in distri-

Table 10
TIMING OF FIRST BIRTHS ACCORDING TO THE RELATIVE AGES OF THE BRIDE AND GROOM: CALIFORNIA BRIDES AGED 15-19: 1966

	Groom's age relative to bride's					
	Younger		Same		Older	
Timing of first birth	N	Percent	N	Percent	N	Percent
0 - 6½ months	440	28.5	1,420	21.9	6,923	16.0
6½ - 8 months	168	10.8	641	9.9	3,432	7.9
8 - 24 months	298	19.3	1,170	18.0	80,503	19.7
no child	640	41.4	3,257	50.2	24,523	56.4
TOTAL	1,546	100.0	6,488	100.0	43,181	100.0

butions to be even less between the younger and older grooms. These expectations are borne out generally by the results, as seen in Table 11. Nonetheless, it appears that even among couples in which the groom is younger than the bride, the older the bride, the less likely she is to have conceived premaritally. It is interesting to note that at age 25, although premarital pregnancy rates are lower than among teenagers, a much higher proportion of premarital conceptions are attributable to brides whose husbands are younger than they are.

Table 11

TIMING OF FIRST BIRTH ACCORDING TO RELATIVE AGES OF THE BRIDE AND GROOM: CALIFORNIA BRIDES AGED 25, 1966

| | Groom's age relative to bride's | | | | | |
| | Younger | | Same | | Older | |
Timing of first birth	N	Percent	N	Percent	N	Percent
0 - 6½ months	36	5.7	15	2.3	74	3.8
6½ - 8 months	17	2.7	10	3.1	55	2.8
8 - 24 months	115	18.1	53	16.1	321	16.6
No child	466	73.5	240	77.9	1,481	76.8
TOTAL	634	100.0	318	100.0	1,931	100.0

$\chi2 = 5.65$

Cramer's $\phi = .03$

For example, among women aged 15-19, only 5 percent of all early premarital conceptions are attributable to brides who married younger men, but among women aged 25, the percentage rises to 29. This point is fairly obvious. First, the older the bride, the more eligible men there are who are younger. Second, teenage boys younger than the bride are probably too young on average to marry easily and are thus less likely than older men to marry a pregnant girl.

In summation: (a) the bride of a younger than of an older husband is more likely to be premaritally pregnant, especially among teenagers; however, (b) the chance that a premaritally pregnant bride will have a husband younger than she is is much greater for older than for teenage women; (c) there are only small differences in postmarital pregnancies according to the relative ages of bride and groom.

These three points lead to the conclusion that older are more likely than younger men to be effective users of contraceptives, assuming that the older are not less active sexually than the younger men.

PREMARITAL PREGNANCIES AND RACE

In Chapter 2 I noted that until very recently there have been substantial differences in the propensity of whites and nonwhites (predominatly blacks) to marry as teenagers. Over time in this country, nonwhite versus white teenagers have exhibited greater rates of marriage (at least for young teenagers), of marital fertility, and of illegitimacy. Saveland and Glick (1969) have estimated first marriage probabilities for whites and nonwhites for the period 1958-1960. Their data indicate that a 15 year old nonwhite woman has a 42 percent greater likelihood of marriage than a 15 year old white woman, and at age 16 a 13 percent greater likelihood. At ages 17-19, whites have slightly higher marriage probabilities than nonwhites.

Illegitimacy is higher among nonwhites than whites. In 1971, among teenagers, the illegitimate birth rate was six times higher for nonwhites than whites in states with laws permitting abortion and ten times higher in states which forbade abortion (Sklar and Berkov, 1974b:911). Marital fertility is also higher among nonwhites. In 1971, ever-married nonwhite women aged 15-44 had borne on average 2.97 children, while ever-married white women had borne 2.26 children (U.S. Bureau of the Census, 1974:113).

Higher rates both of marriage and of illegitimacy should lead to higher rates of premarital conceptions among nonwhites than among whites. Generally, the California data follow this expectation. (The reader is referred to Appendix C for a technical discussion of the way in which data by race were generated for the California marriage cohort of 1966.) Among the early conceivers there is not much difference by race at age 15, with 49 percent of the nonwhite brides and 45 percent of the white brides being pregnant. But, at every other age group up to age 30, the percentage of nonwhite brides who were pregnant is quite a bit higher than that of white brides (see Table 12).

Regardless of race, the gradient by age is fairly steep. For example, from age 15 to age 19, there is a decline of 29 percentage points for nonwhites, and a decline of 18 percentage points between ages 19 and the oldest age group considered, 35-44. For whites, the gradient is even steeper within the teen years, with a decline of 34 percentage points between ages 15 and 19, and a decline of only 9 percentage points between ages 19 and 35-44. Overall, however, the chi-square values suggest greater variation by age among nonwhites than among whites.

Between six and a half and eight months after marriage, births tend to occur to a higher percentage of whites than nonwhites, although the differences are not large. This suggests that whites marry sooner than nonwhites after the discovery of a pregnancy. If a birth during the first eight months after marriage is used as a more liberal definition of premarital pregnancies, the data reveal, of course, higher incidences, but essentially the same pattern by age and race. Overall, between marriage and eight months after, 23 percent of the nonwhites and 17 percent of the whites were pregnant at marriage. Of the women married at age 15, 54 percent of the nonwhites and 60 percent of the white brides were pregnant. By age 19, the respective percentages had dropped to 25 and 17, for net percentage declines of 54 and 72. By ages 35-44 the figures were 3 percent for each category, showing a percentage decline from age 19 of 88 for nonwhites and 82 for whites.

The data for California are consistent with a similar type of analysis using data from Massachusetts in 1966-1968

Table 12

RACIAL DIFFERENCES IN PREMARITAL PREGNANCIES BY AGE AT FIRST MARRIAGE: CALIFORNIA MARRIAGE COHORT, 1966 (IN PERCENT)

| Age at first marriage | Births within months of marriage | | | | | |
| | 6½ | | 6½ - 8 | | 8 | |
	White	Nonwhite	White	Nonwhite	White	Nonwhite
15	44.6	48.5	15.4	5.4	60.0	53.9
16	28.8	44.4	13.6	8.1	42.4	52.5
17	24.2	36.3	12.2	7.9	36.4	44.2
18	14.1	28.9	8.1	7.2	22.2	36.1
19	10.6	19.8	6.7	5.3	17.3	25.1
20	8.3	15.3	5.2	4.6	13.5	19.9
21	5.9	10.9	4.5	5.0	10.4	15.9
22-24	4.8	9.8	3.3	4.8	8.1	14.6
25-29	4.0	7.2	2.6	4.3	6.6	11.5
30-34	3.8	2.6	2.6	1.0	6.4	3.6
35-44	1.8	2.2	1.1	0.9	2.9	3.1
TOTAL	11.0	17.9	6.4	5.3	17.4	23.2
χ^2	171.5	157.5	37.7	11.0	66.9	78.5
N(Women at Risk)[a]	91,383	10,847	88,629	10,754		

[a]Data are adjusted for migration.

[Whelan, 1972b] . Whelan had data only for mothers, not for all brides, but her data indicate that 72 percent of all legitimate first births to nonwhites aged 15-19 were conceived premaritally versus 60 percent of white births. Further, her data indicate that whites tend to marry sooner after pregnancy than do nonwhites.

PREMARITAL PREGNANCIES AND ETHNICITY

As an ethnic group, Mexican-Americans represent the second largest minority group in the United States. In California they in fact outnumber blacks and are that state's largest minority group. Like blacks, the Mexican-American population has been characterized demographically by high teenage nuptiality and fertility, but their illegitimacy data are not currently available.

On the basis of data from the California Department of Public Health, I have calculated that 1966 marriage rates among 15 year old Mexican-American women were 93 percent higher than for all 15 year old women, 41 percent higher at age 16, 24 percent higher at age 17, and achieved approximate parity with the total population at ages 18-19.

Fertility levels among Mexican-Americans have also been historically high. In both the 1960 and 1970 censuses, the number of children ever born *at any age* is higher for the Mexican-American population than for either the black or Anglo (non-Mexican-American white) populations. However, in the absence of data on illegitimacy among Mexican-Americans it would be difficult to know whether to expect low levels of premarital pregnancy because women tend to marry early and bear children postmaritally, or whether early marriage is a product of high levels of illegitimate conceptions, or both.

For births occurring during the first eight months of marriage, the data in Table 13 indicate that 22 percent of all Mexican-American marriages were of pregnant brides, compared to 16 percent of the Anglo couples. However, the Mexican-Americans have lower rates of premarital pregnancy at age 15 than is true for the rest of the brides and there is little difference at age 16. The higher overall rate of premarital pregnancies for Mexican-Americans is produced by a widening of the differentials between Mexican-American and Anglo brides through the late teens and early twenties. From age 18 through ages 22-34 Mexican-Americans sustain a level of premarital pregnancy at least 28 percent higher than the Anglo brides.

Table 13

PREMARITAL PREGNANCIES AMONG MEXICAN-AMERICANS: CALIFORNIA MARRIAGE COHORT, 1966 (IN PERCENT)

Age at first marriage	Births within months of marriage					
	6½		6½ - 8		8	
	Mex-Amer.	Anglo	Mex-Amer.	Anglo	Mex-Amer.	Anglo
15 and younger	43.8	46.2	9.1	18.5	52.9	64.7
16	31.6	28.7	10.6	14.5	42.2	43.2
17	30.2	23.4	9.1	13.0	39.3	36.4
18	22.5	12.8	9.8	8.4	29.3	21.2
19	16.0	9.8	6.3	6.7	22.3	16.5
20	14.0	7.3	4.8	5.1	18.8	12.4
21	12.4	4.8	5.0	4.3	17.4	9.1
22-24	9.2	4.0	4.1	3.0	13.3	7.0
25-29	7.3	3.1	2.4	2.7	9.7	5.8
30-34	5.3	3.2	1.9	2.9	7.2	6.1
35-44	2.7	1.3	0.0	1.6	2.7	2.9
TOTAL	16.6	10.0	5.6	6.4	22.2	16.4

Of perhaps even greater interest is the finding that Mexican-American, like nonwhite couples, are more likely than the rest to be early premarital conceivers, that is, to bear a child during the first six and a half months of marriage. At most ages they are less likely than the rest to be late premarital conceivers, that is, to bear a child between six and a half and eight months after marriage. The inference is that Mexican-Americans, and nonwhites (see Table 12), are perhaps more prone to let the discovery of pregnancy dictate the timing of marriage, rather than letting the date of marriage dictate the onset of uncontrolled pregnancy. There is less variation by age in premarital pregnancies among Mexican-Americans than is true for the rest of the brides, although a steep age gradient is still present, particularly among the early premarital conceivers.

A comparison of Tables 12 and 13 shows that Mexican-American teenagers have lower rates of premarital pregnancies than do nonwhites, yet in all likelihood Mexican-American teenagers have much higher marriage rates. It thus seems reasonable to conclude that teenage illegitimate fertility among Mexican-Americans is considerably less than among blacks. However, marital fertility is almost certainly higher for Mexican-Americans.

HOW LIKELY IS A PREMARITAL PREGNANCY?

It is easy to get lost in large percentages at young ages and come out with the feeling that an incredibly high proportion of teenage women are having babies and getting married. In fact, the numbers are large, but they are declining. By converting the marriage rates from Figure 4 to probabilities, and applying period data to standard life-table procedures, I have calculated that in California in 1966 there was a 39 percent chance that a 15 year old girl would be married before she turned 20. This is exactly the same result as if age-specific marriage rates were cumulated between 1966 and 1970. The latter method is an approximation of cohort data. In 1973 the probability that a 15 year old girl would marry by age 20 had dropped to 24 percent, using the life-table probability technique. Insufficient data were available to make a cohort estimate.

In 1966 there was a 10 percent chance that a 15 year old girl would become a pregnant bride before reaching 20. But, if we assume the same likelihood of a premarital pregnancy as in 1966, then by 1973 the declines in marriage probabilities alone meant that a girl at 15 had only a 6 percent chance of becoming a pregnant bride before reaching age 20. These probabilities are slightly higher for blacks and lower for whites. Although the probabilities are fairly low of being a pregnant bride, in 1966 in California a 15 year old girl faced a 34 per-cent chance of bearing at least one child (legitimately or illegitimately) before reaching age 20. Since premarital preg-nancies are such an important facet of teenage marriages, the next chapter turns to a consideration of some of the social and economic factors related to the changes over time in the incidence of premarital pregnancies among teenagers, as well as among older women.

5

HISTORICAL CHANGES IN PREMARITAL PREGNANCIES

A woman's ability to conceive and bear children generally peaks during the late teens and early twenties and declines after that. A knowledge of birth preventing measures tends to be greatest a few years after marriage. Thus, the existence of illegitimacy and premarital conceptions should not be surprising in any society in which marriages are delayed past puberty. Indeed, it is indicative of the strength of social norms that illegitimacy and premarital pregnancies throughout the world are as few in number as they are. It should not surprise us that the incidences seem to increase when major social and economic changes are occurring.

HISTORICAL PATTERN OF PREMARITAL PREGNANCIES

Historians have recently begun to uncover evidence which suggests that European cultures long have been characterized by the noticeable existence of pregnant brides. Although data are thinly and widely scattered, the possible relationship between changes in the incidence of premarital pregnancies and concurrent social changes suggests the thesis that premarital

pregnancies signal transitions in family structure occasioned
by broader social and economic alterations in society.

Hair has analyzed records from rural parishes in England
covering a period of history from 1538 to 1807 [Hair, 1970].
His data reveal a range among pregnant brides from a low of
3 percent in Orwell parish between 1600 and 1619 to a high
of 49 percent in Medmenham parish between 1750 and 1836.
Overall, roughly one-fifth of the brides covered in the sample
of eighteen parishes from 1538 to 1700 and two-fifths from
1700 to 1836 bore a child within eight and a half months of
marriage, the cutoff date Hair set for determining a premarital
conception. Laslett [1965] has produced the only other
historical data on premarital conceptions for England. His
figures show an incidence range from a low of 13 percent in
Clayworth parish in 1650-1750 to a high of 34 percent in
Wyle parish in 1654-1783.

At first glance, these data seem only to say that premarital
pregnancies are more common in recent years than earlier.
However, I think that another reasonable interpretation of
the data is that the increases may be associated with family
disorganization occurring during the inaugural years of the
industrial revolution in England. Cipolla [1965] notes that
the period of initial industrialization in England was 1760-
1790, and Smelser [1959] has documented some of the
family changes wrought by industrialization. Hair's data on
premarital pregnancies show that prior to 1750 the highest
percentage of brides pregnant in any parish was 30 percent,
whereas between 1750 and 1807 (the end limit of Hair's data)
four out of six parishes show percentages higher than 30 and
three of those are 40 percent or more. It thus seems reasonable to speculate that changes in rural social organization
which may have been occurring as preliminaries to industrialization were creating a certain level of family disorganization,
reflected in increasing rates of premarital pregnancies.

This general model of social change and premarital pregnancies seems also to fit the data for Anhausen, Germany, published by Knodel [1970]. Knodel reconstituted family histories for that southern German village, and found that 14 percent of the brides between 1692-1749 were pregnant, 17 percent between 1750-1799, 20 percent between 1800-1849, but dropped back to 14 percent between 1850-1899. If illegitimate births are added to the premarital pregnancies, the differences for each period are even more marked. For each of the above four periods of time, the percent of all first births conceived outside of marriage were, respectively, 16, 22, 38, and 27. The peak was therefore reached during the period 1800-1849. Knodel relates these changes over time to restrictive marriage laws. Yet, these legal changes were not operating in a vacuum. Cipolla cites Germany as undergoing the initial stages of industrialization in roughly the 1830-1870 period, which is approximately the same time interval during which premarital pregnancies peaked in Anhausen.

For the United States, Demos [1968] reports that in the community of Bristol, Rhode Island, there was an increase in the incidence of premarital pregnancies from none in 1680-1720 to 10 percent in 1720-1740, to 49 percent in 1740-1760, and to 44 percent in 1760-1780. These latter two figures are remarkably similar to those for that same period of time in rural England (see Hair's data above). Of more importance, however, is that the rise in premarital pregnancies seems to be associated with an increase in commercial activity in Bristol, accompanied by a rise in the sex ratio in the adult ages. This was also the time of the American Revolution which, in conjunction with changes in the economic structure, was quite clearly a factor in that period's social change.

It is of course currently the case that teenagers bear a majority of premaritally conceived children, and that the percentage of pregnant teenage brides is considerably higher than for older women. Yet, in none of the historical studies discussed are teenagers implicated as the primary source of premarital pregnancies. After examing the parish for which he had the greatest amount of relevant data, Hair [1970:65] concluded that in rural England, "bridal pregnancy was clearly not due to teenage innocence. Another inference from the Medmenham figures is that there was little teenage promiscuity." Laslett presents no data on the age of pregnant brides, but Knodel has some data for Anhausen, Germany. For the entire period from 1692-1939, Knodel [1970:397] found that the highest incidence of premarital pregnancy was among women aged 22-24 (23 percent), followed by ages below 22 (16 percent), ages 30 and over (15 percent), and finally ages 25-29 (13 percent).

Apparently, then, the greater prevalence of premarital pregnancies among teenagers than among older women which we currently find in the United States (and in England as well) represents a shift over time in behavior patterns. As the distribution of brides has shifted downward in age, the teenage years have come to be in the mainstream of nuptiality behavior, particularly since World War II. In 1959, the United States Census Bureau conducted a survey in which marital and fertility histories were collected from a national sample of women. The data from this study indicate that before World War II there was little change in the percentage of white women who were pregnant at marriage (measured by births during the first eight months of marriage). During the 44 year period from the turn of the century to 1944, pregnant brides ranged from a low of 7 percent to a high of 9 percent. However, the post-World War II period evidenced a rapid increase in the incidence of premarital pregnancy. For whites, a 100 percent increase in the proportion of pregnant brides was observed between 1940-1944 (8 percent) and 1955-1959 (16 percent). The rapid rate of economic expansion and concomitant social changes certainly were closely tied to these changes in premarital conceptions.

In Figure 9 are plotted the changes over time in premarital pregnancies (for all ages) and the percentages of teenagers who were married. The latter percentage increased markedly during the forties and subsequently decreased. It appears to be generally true that as the proportion of married teenagers declined, the incidence of premarital pregnancy increased. This suggests that not until after World War II did teenagers begin to dominate statistics on premarital pregnancies.

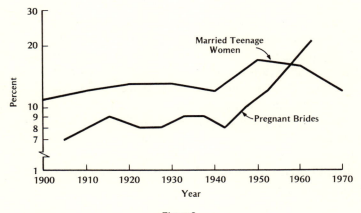

Figure 9
PERCENTAGE OF TEENAGE WOMEN WHO WERE MARRIED
AND PERCENTAGE OF BRIDES (ALL AGES) WITH A PREMARITAL
PREGNANCY (ALL AGES), UNITED STATES, 1900-1969, WHITES ONLY

If the timing of social change and shifting levels of pre-marital pregnancies are more than a coincidence, what then might explain the linkages between the two? Specifically, how could social changes of one type or another be translated into an alteration of premarital sexual behavior or a change in nuptiality? The answer seems to lie in social control. During periods of social change, the normative structure of society tends to break down, as new modes of behavior are accom-modated and old modes of behavior are questioned. Once a norm is questioned, the power of enforcement of that norm tends to be severely reduced. Since adult males and females have a virtually universal desire to engage in sexual activity, it should not be surprising that norms regarding sexual be-havior are sensitive to other shifts in the normative order. This is particularly true since sexual activity is generally very private and hard to regulate even under the best of circumstances.

For the post-World War II period, the evidence seems fairly convincing that increases in premarital pregnancies have been associated with increasing sexual activity on the part of the unmarried population, particularly among the young. A study in Michigan by Vener and Stewart [1974] suggested that pre-marital sexuality among adolescents was related to the use of illicit drugs, alcohol, and cigarettes. If we couple that finding with Kantner and Zelnick's data [1972b] indicating a 50 per-cent chance that a girl will engage in premarital intercourse before age 19, the breakdown in social control during the sixties and early seventies is quite striking. Demographically, this breakdown is evidenced by a rise in premarital sexual activity among teenagers.

PREMARITAL SEXUAL ACTIVITY

Most people are willing to acknowledge on faith the fact that there has indeed been an increase over time in premarital sexual activity. The opinion has been raised, however, that there has not really been any change over time, but rather that premarital sexual activity used to be covert, whereas now it is more overt. The latter argument seems to miss the point, however, that overt behavior is more likely to pick up adher-ents at the margin than is covert behavior. Furthermore, it is a position weakened by findings such as those of Cannon and

Long that "there has not been a single major study that has been done in the late sixties that has found premarital coital rates that were the low level of those found in the late 1950s and early 1960s" [Cannon and Long, 1971:36]. An example of such a study is Christensen and Gregg [1970] who reported that whereas in 1958 less than 10 percent of the Utah teenage women sampled had experienced premarital coitus, 32 percent had had such an experience in the 1968 sample.

Several studies done during the fifties [e.g., Kain and Howard, 1958; Burgess and Wallis, 1953] reported fairly high (around 45 percent) proportions of respondents who admitted to having had premarital sexual experiences. But these studies also tended to corroborate Kinsey's thesis that premarital sexual activity was class-bound behavior—practiced more widely in lower class settings than in the higher classes [see Kain and Howard, 1958, for a fuller discussion]. One explanation for this fact is that the lower classes had less to lose in terms of economic security and social prestige than did the middle or upper classes. Thus they were more likely to act out frustrations in interpersonal relations by behaving in "deviant" ways, such as engaging in premarital and extra-marital sexual activity, and being more willing to dissolve a marriage. Also ethnographic studies, such as Liebow's *Tally's Corner* have illustrated that conditions of poverty may result in failure in the established institutions such as marriage, and that under these conditions individuals may seek alternative modes of behavior which redefine failure and success. Thus, a teenage girl who is pregnant at her wedding might be labeled a "success" because she had proven her womanhood, rather than labeled a failure because she had engaged in premarital sexual activity and been caught. What appears to be happening currently, however, is that premarital sexuality and related behavior patterns are becoming more common and less class bound [Kantner and Zelnick, 1972a].

Earlier writers on the subject generally assumed a stable

model of society, in which there was a constant level of sexual activity among teenagers. Under this model, as the marriage rate went down, illegitimacy went up and vice-versa [see, e.g., Pohlman, 1969]. However, recent increases in premarital pregnancies have come at a time when the age at marriage has been declining. While the not-so-easily regulated norms regarding sexual activity have been increasingly called into question, the more easily enforced regulations concerning the dispensing of contraceptive information and appliances to teenagers have been slower to change. The result has been an increase in uncontrolled sexual activity on the part of the young, resulting in higher levels of illegitimate conceptions and teenage nuptials.

TEENAGE USE OF CONTRACEPTION

An unfortunate aspect of the rise in premarital sexual activity among teenagers is their relatively infrequent use of contraceptives. Symptomatic of the relative non-use of birth prevention measures is the study in Baltimore by Furstenburg, Gordis, and Markowitz [1969], in which only 41 percent of a sample of 167 unmarried pregnant teenagers had ever used birth control. Another study of black teenagers in Winston-Salem, North Carolina, revealed that there was an average lag of seven months between first intercourse and first use of a contraceptive [Vincent, Harvey, and Cochrane, 1969]. Among women in their 1971 national sample, Kantner and Zelnick [1972a] found that less than 20 percent of the sexually experienced 15-19 year olds always used some method of birth control. They also discovered that among unmarried teenagers, the most frequently mentioned method of contraception was the condom [Kantner and Zelnick, 1973]. This method requires motivation on the part of the male, not the female, and its use may be more to protect against venereal disease than to protect against pregnancy. Their data indicate that the shift to the use of the pill as a contraceptive generally comes after marriage when, for many women, it is already too late to prevent the first pregnancy.

An important reason for the lack of contraceptive utilization among teenagers is lack of information. In New York City, Presser [1974] found that only 19 percent of the teenage mothers even knew when during the month they were most at risk of pregnancy. Indeed, the low level of knowledge undoubtedly goes a long way toward explaining why those teenagers became mothers. I asked the same question of a sample of 73 never-pregnant, never-married teenage women in San Diego and found that two-thirds of the women who had engaged in sexual activity could correctly identify the period of greatest pregnancy risk, while half of the never sexually active women could make the correct identification [Weeks, 1975]. Since 70 percent of the women were 18-19 year olds, and most were college students, the level of knowledge is still disconcertingly low.

Even though there may be a strong relationship between lack of sexual knowledge and the likelihood of premarital pregnancy, it is nonetheless true that Americans are not overwhelmingly in favor of providing birth control services to teenage girls. Blake [1973] found that in 1969, 35 percent of American women and 50 percent of American men favored the provision of such services. Approval had increased by 1972 to 61 percent among women and 62 percent among men, but that still leaves nearly 40 percent opposing birth control services to teenagers.

Premarital pregnancies are not the only problematic aspect of teenage marriages. As we shall see in the next chapter, teenagers are also more likely than older women to have a postmarital conception early in marriage even if they were not pregnant at marriage.

6
POSTMARITALLY CONCEIVED BIRTHS

In Chapters 4 and 5 we saw that teenage marriages differ markedly from marriages of older women in terms of premaritally conceived births. Even within the teen years there are considerable differences. But what of the marriages that occurred without the early birth of a child? In this chapter we will look at births conceived after the marriage took place. The discussion will necessarily focus on the first two years of marriage since data for California were not available beyond that.

Let us first examine data for women married in 1965-1969 in the United States. Among brides aged 14-18, 15 percent had a child between eight and twelve months after marriage compared to about 12 percent for brides aged 19-21 (see Table 14). Since premarital conceptions were defined as those births between zero and eight months after marriage, the inclusion of the eighth month of marriage may also include some premaritally conceived births. There is virtually no difference in the percentage of 14-18 and 19-21 year old brides who had their first child during the second year of marriage.

The data for the California marriage cohort of 1966 are

similar to those for the entire United States. The percentage
of brides whose first matched birth was postmaritally conceived is not very different for teenagers and older women.
The differences between premarital and postmarital conceivers are shown in Table 15. If we look first at the percentage of women at each age who bore their first child during
the eighth through the twelfth months of their first year of
marriage, we find that the steep gradient has virtually dis-
appeared. As the very low values of chi-square suggest, there
is little in the way of a discernible pattern in the percentage

Table 14

**EARLY PREMARITAL BIRTHS BY AGE AT MARRIAGE:
WOMEN MARRIED BETWEEN 1965-1969, UNITED STATES
(IN PERCENT)**

Age at first marriage	Months between marriage and first birth:		
	0-8	8-12	12-24
14-18	28.8	15.2	27.1
19-21	17.0	11.6	27.9
22+	16.3	11.1	22.4

Source: Calculated from U.S. Bureau of Census, 1974:55.

of women whose first child after marriage was born during
the eighth through twelfth months of marriage. It is true,
however, that women married at ages 17 and 18 exhibit a
slightly higher than average incidence of children born during
this period, whereas women married at ages 21-24, and women
aged 35-44 exhibit a somewhat lower than average incidence
of childbearing during this period.

　　The differences between the late teens and early to mid-
twenties are even more muted when births during the second

year of marriage are considered. Our data do not cover the full second year of marriage for the entire cohort, but the data should be indicative. In Table 15 it can be seen that there is very little variation by age at first marriage in the percentage of women who bear their first child during the second year of marriage. Only at the oldest age group, 35-44, is there an appreciable deviation from normal, and we can attribute the low percentage at that age probably as much to low fecundity by this age as to a reproduction motivation different from that of younger brides. At first glance, then, it appears that the differences in age in the timing of first births among brides is due almost entirely to differences in premarital conceptions.

Table 15

EARLY POSTMARITAL BIRTHS, BY AGE AT FIRST MARRIAGE: CALIFORNIA, 1966 (IN PERCENT)

Age at first marriage	Months between marriage and first birth:		
	8-12	13-24	8-24
15	9.7	10.2	19.9
16	11.4	11.1	22.5
17	11.7	10.7	22.4
18	12.0	11.0	23.0
19	9.9	10.7	20.6
20	10.1	9.9	20.0
21	8.5	9.7	18.2
22-24	8.6	8.7	17.3
25-29	10.4	10.3	20.7
30-34	10.9	8.8	19.7
35-44	4.4	4.5	8.9
TOTAL	10.1	10.0	20.1
χ^2	4.6	3.8	5.1
N(Women at Risk)[a]	96,636	90,508	

aData adjusted for migration.

MEASURING THE RISK OF A POSTMARITALLY CONCEIVED CHILD

It is possible that the data in Tables 14 and 15 for the United States and California are misleading since they are based on percentages of all brides rather than pregnant brides only. Since pregnant brides tend to swell the ranks of the married at the young ages, their presence will tend to deflate the relative importance of postmarital conceptions of young brides compared to older brides. We should base our calculations on only those brides who have not yet had a child, thus asking what percentage of brides who did not bear a child conceived premaritally will bear a postmaritally conceived child early in marriage. The results of such calculations are shown in Table 16 and indicate that a considerable age gradient does in fact exist among postmaritally conceived births just as it did for premaritally conceived births. The younger the teenager, the greater is the likelihood of a postmaritally conceived child being born either 8-12 or 12-24 months after marriage. For example, among the women who were 17 when they married and who were still childless after a full year of marriage, there was a 21.8 percent chance that a child would be born during the next 12 months. Yet, among women aged 22-24 when married, who were still childless after a year, there was only a 10.4 percent chance that a child would be born in the second year of marriage. Above age 19 there is less variation in the birth rate than at age 19 and below, as was true for premaritally conceived births.

The data suggest, then, that teenage brides are much more likely to become mothers early in marriage than are older brides, even if they were not pregnant at marriage. Since the "older" brides refers, for example, to women of ages 20-24—women still in their prime period of fecundity—the differences in the incidences of motherhood by age cannot reasonably be ascribed to differences by age in the ability of women to conceive and bear a live child. Rather, the differences must be accounted for by differences in the use of contraceptives, or abortion. However, therapeutic abortions were still largely illegal in California in the period in question, so it is not possible to assess its importance in these age differences.

When examining births according to the brides who were actually at risk of bearing a postmaritally conceived child, we should note that some of those marriages may represent cases in which the bride was pregnant but had an abortion (either spontaneously or by induction), or in which the marriage followed rather than preceded, the birth of the child. Reports of fetal deaths among teenagers vary in the literature from a low

Table 16

**POSTMARITALLY CONCEIVED BIRTHS BY AGE AT MARRIAGE:
CALIFORNIA
(IN PERCENT)**

Age at marriage	Months between marriage and birth:	
	8-11	12-24
15	25.3	37.9
16	20.8	26.0
17	19.0	21.8
18	15.8	17.1
19	12.3	14.9
20	11.8	13.0
21	9.6	12.0
22-24	9.4	10.4
25-29	11.2	12.3
30-34	11.6	10.4
35-44	4.6	4.7
TOTAL	12.4	14.0
χ^2	30.0	64.8
N (Women at risk)[a]	78,471	65,064

[a]Data adjusted for migration.

of 1 percent of all pregnancies [Shapiro, et al., 1968:321] to a high of 8 percent [Day, 1967:180]. Another study [Weeks, 1972], indicates that no more than 2 percent of the brides at any age were marrying a man whose illegitimate child they had born within the 90 days prior to marriage. Thus, the number of teenage brides who either were pregnant at marriage but did not bear a live child or who might not have been at risk of pregnancy at the time of marriage because of a recent birth would represent, at a maximum, about 4 percent.

IMPLICATIONS OF EARLY CHILDBEARING

A major implication of the patterns of early marital child-bearing among teenagers is that legitimate fertility rates will be disproportionately affected by teenagers if they are having their children sooner after marriage than older brides. Of course, the impact of teenage fertility on the total fertility of a population is a function of several variables. Most important-ly, it depends upon the distribution of marriages, since only within marriage is full sexual activity (and implicitly repro-duction) likely to occur during the teen years. Yaukey (1973) has pointed out that higher ages at marriage tend to be asso-ciated with lower overall fertility at the young ages, even where illegitimacy is high. The latter point is true because illegitimate rates are almost never as high as legitimate fertility rates. This is certainly true in California, as the reader can note by refer-ring to Figure 7.

The impact of teenage fertility on the total population also depends upon child-spacing and completed family size. If wom-en bear many children on an average over their lifetime, then other things being equal, the contribution made during the teen years will be small in comparison to overall levels of fer-tility. If children are born in rapid succession, then an early age at marriage is likely to be accompanied by higher levels of procreative activity during the teen years than if the normal pattern is for fairly long intervals between children.

Within the California marriage cohort of 1966, teenage women were bearing children earlier within marriage than older women, and as a consequence, there was a slight tendency for teenage women to be more likely to bear a second matched legitimate child than is true for older women, regardless of the timing of the first birth (see Table 17). In general, however, the number of second births is too small to attribute much significance to differences in the percentages of women having a second birth. It is interesting, nonetheless, to observe that 18 year olds show by far the biggest differences in second-birth probabilities according to the timing of the first birth. Thus for 18 year old women whose first birth was postmaritally conceived, the incidence of a second birth is less than for

Table 17

SECOND BIRTH FOLLOWING FIRST MATCHED BIRTH

| | Was Conceived | | | | | |
| | Premaritally | | | Postmaritally | | |
Age at first marriage	Number of women	Number of second births	Percent	Number of women	Number of second births	Percent
15	545	41	7.5	146	4	2.7
16	2,082	155	7.4	962	13	1.4
17	3,220	231	7.2	1,748	24	1.4
18	2,726	250	9.2	3,544	30	0.8
19	3,177	173	5.4	3,155	20	0.6
20	1,689	93	5.5	2,010	26	1.3
21	1,114	56	5.0	1,516	7	0.5
22-24	1,545	67	4.3	2,415	24	1.0
25-29	601	22	3.7	1,211	13	1.1
30-34	140	8	5.7	313	4	1.3
35-44	52	0	0.0	86	0	0.0
TOTALS	16,891	1,096	6.5	17,106	165	1.0
χ^2			10.7			4.9

teenagers as a group. Yet, among those 18 year olds whose
first pregnancy was premarital, the incidence of a second
matched birth is higher than for teenagers as a group. Again,
the numbers are small and we do not want to overestimate the
importance of differences, but the implication is that pregnant teenage brides have less motivation to practice family
limitation or fertility control than do older women.

We can conclude, then, that teenagers are not only more
likely than older brides to bear a premaritally conceived child,
but also more likely to bear a first and then a second postmaritally conceived child. We should also note, however, that
since illegitimacy rates were fairly high in California in 1966-
1967, not all of the first matched births are the actual first
births to these women.

FIRST LIVE BIRTHS AND FIRST MATCHED BIRTHS COMPARED

To what extent is a first matched birth also the first live
birth to a mother? Table 18 summarizes the data, where it
can be seen that for births occurring within six and one half
months after marriage, a very high percentage to teenagers
were first live births, as would be expected. Or, they may not
have reported a previous pregnancy, a possibility that cannot
be ruled out. After age 20, however, the percentages tend to
drop off until age 35-44 where fewer than two-thirds of all
first matched births were also first live births. The older a
woman becomes, apparently the more likely it is that she has
either had a child before marriage, or has not admitted on the
marriage certificate to previous marriages.

When we look at late premarital pregnancies we find higher
percentages of first matched births which are also first live
births than for women with early premarital pregnancies, especially at older ages. This pattern seems reasonable. We
might well expect women who became pregnant only shortly
before marriage to have had lower levels of premarital sexual
experience than women whose pregnancy occurred well before

marriage. Following through with this line of reasoning would lead us to expect even higher percentages of first matched births conceived postmaritally to be also first live births to women. Our expectations are borne out at the oldest ages (30-44), as can be seen in Table 18, but not among teenagers. The teenage postmarital conceivers are slightly more likely to have a child prior to marriage than the early premarital conceivers. Some of the women represent those discussed earlier who were at low risk of a premarital pregnancy because they had recently borne an illegitimate child. We should note also that some of the discrepancy between first live births and first matched births may be due to errors inherent in the record linkage process. Appendix A contains a fuller discussion of that issue.

With the incidence and timing of live births within teenage marriages already examined, it is time to discuss a problem that follows some live births, the incidence of infant mortality.

Table 18

**FIRST MATCHED BIRTHS THAT ARE FIRST LIVE BIRTHS:
BY AGE OF BRIDE AT FIRST MARRIAGE: CALIFORNIA, 1966
(IN PERCENT)**

Age at first marriage	First matched, first live births within months of marriage		
	6½	6½ - 8	8-24
15	96.2	98.4	86.3
16	95.2	96.6	90.0
17	94.2	96.6	89.8
18	93.7	95.5	92.9
19	93.8	96.4	91.7
20	91.1	91.7	90.3
21	85.7	92.3	90.0
22-24	82.2	86.8	86.9
25-29	72.9	84.9	82.8
30-34	53.5	70.3	82.5
35-44	57.6	68.4	76.3
TOTAL	91.5	93.9	89.5

7

INFANT MORTALITY

Infant mortality rates tend to be higher for children born to teenage than to mothers of other ages [see the discussion in Chapter 1, as well as NCHS, 1973; Day, 1967; Heady and Morris, 1959; Gerard and Hemery, 1973]. Among all babies born in the United States in 1960, infant mortality rates were 31 percent higher for children of mothers aged 15-19 than for children of mothers of all ages, and 43 percent higher than for children of mothers aged 25-29 [NCHS, 1973:4]. Only among children of mothers aged 45 or older were infant mortality rates higher than for those to teenage mothers.

Infant mortality rates also are higher among illegitimate children than legitimate children [NCHS, 1973; Gerard and Hemery, 1973; Chase and Nelson, 1973]. Infant mortality rates for white illegitimate and total children by mother's age for the United States in 1960 are shown in Table 19. Rates are highest for illegitimate children of women over 29, followed by illegitimate children of teenagers. Overall, the risk of death is greater for illegitimate children than for legitimate regardless of the mother's age. Chase and Nelson [1973] drew a similar conclusion from New York City.

Since infant mortality rates appear to be related both to

mother's age and legitimacy status, it is reasonable to expect that premaritally conceived (i.e., illegitimately conceived) births will be associated with higher infant mortality rates than postmaritally conceived births. Premarital pregnancies tend to be associated with economic instability (Coombs and Freedman, 1970) as well as with marital instability (see Chapter 8). Thus, we should expect to find children conceived out of wedlock disproportionately exposed to the risk of death even

Table 19

INFANT MORTALITY RATES FOR ILLEGITIMATE
AND TOTAL LIVE BIRTHS, BY AGE OF MOTHER:
UNITED STATES, 1960, WHITES ONLY

Age of mother	Rate per 1,000 live births		
	Illegitimate (1)	Total (2)	Ratio (1 ÷ 2)
15-19	33.0	28.1	1.17
20-24	30.3	21.4	1.41
25-29	32.7	20.0	1.63
30+	39.0	22.3	1.74
TOTAL	33.0	22.2	1.49

Source: NCHS, 1973.

though born legitimately. Economic and marital instability tend to lead to social situations in which the health of the young is neglected or, in the case of child abuse, actually threatened. We should find this to be true of all ages, but particularly for teenagers. For them a premarital pregnancy is more likely to lead to a forced and unwanted marriage than for older women.

In the literature I have found only one study which relates

infant mortality to conception status. Stewart [1959] indicates that among a group of married primiparae (women having their first child) in England in 1952, the perinatal death rates (the sum of stillbirths and neonatal deaths) were two to three times higher for premarital than for postmarital conceptions. The smallest difference was for housewives and the largest for working women. Although her findings were in the expected direction, Stewart's study provided neither data on the age of the mother nor insights into factors which might explain the difference.

New data on infant mortality by conception status were obtained for this study from the linkage of marriages, births, and infant deaths in California. Data refer to all births matched from the day of marriage up to the second wedding anniversary. Since records were matched by calendar year whereas the marriage anniversary is measured from the date of marriage, a marriage contracted on 1 January 1966 was followed for a full two years whereas a marriage contracted on 31 December 1966 was followed for only one year.

INFANT MORTALITY RATES

There were 36, 959 first live births matched in the calendar years 1966 and 1967 to the 107,676 first marriages contracted in California in calendar year 1966. Of these live births, 638 died during the first year of life. This is equivalent to an infant mortality rate of 17.3 per 1,000 or slightly less than the rate of 19.8 per 1,000 averaged for California from 1966-1968. This is normal, however, since more than 90 percent of the first matched births to brides in this study were also first-order births, and the risk of infant mortality is less for first-order than for higher-order births [NCHS, 1973]. Data for the United States for 1960 suggest that the ratio of the mortality rate for first-order births to the rate for all births is .85. Since the ratio of the mortality rate for my data to that for the state as a whole is .87 we can assume that my data generally represent the infant mortality situation in California in 1966-1968.

INFANT MORTALITY AND PREMARITAL PREGNANCY

The proposition that infant mortality (deaths per 1,000 live births) is related to the timing of a pregnancy after marriage is supported by the data in Table 20. Infant mortality rates are almost twice as high for babies born during the first six and one-half months of marriage as for babies born eight months or later after marriage. Note that babies born within the six weeks occurring between six and one half and eight months after marriage may or may not have been conceived premaritally, and the low infant mortality rates may be a product of a small number of infant deaths rather than being substantively significant. Babies born during this interval after marriage have been excluded

Table 20

INFANT MORTALITY RATES BY TIMING OF BIRTH AFTER MARRIAGE, AND AGE OF MOTHER: CALIFORNIA MARRIAGE COHORT, 1966

Age of mother	Infant mortality rates by time of conceptions		
	Early premarital[a]	Late premarital[b]	Postmarital[c]
15-17	28.0 (4,101)[d]	5.2 (1,746)	12.6 (2,941)
18-19	21.6 (4,682)	9.2 (2,495)	9.8 (7,030)
20-21	26.3 (1,748)	15.2 (1,055)	18.9 (3,871)
22+	34.7 (1,442)	16.7 (897)	17.3 (4,852)
TOTAL	26.1 (11,973)	10.2 (6,193)	14.1 (18,694)

[a]Child born during 0-6½ months after marriage.
[b]Child born 6½-8 months after marriage.
[c]Child born 8+ months after marriage.
[d]Numbers in parentheses refer to total number of births.

from the analysis in order more clearly to compare premarital with postmarital conceptions.

Infant mortality rates among early premaritally conceived children are 47 to 59 percent higher than the overall rates for each age category, whereas infant mortality rates for postmaritally conceived children are 12 to 31 percent lower than average for each age category.

Table 21

RATIO OF MORTALITY RATES FOR EACH PREGNANCY STATUS GROUP FOR COMBINED PREGNANCY STATUSES IN EACH AGE GROUP

Age of mother	Early premarital pregnancy	Postmarital pregnancy	Total
15-17	1.53	.69	1.00
18-19	1.59	.72	1.00
20+	1.47	.88	1.00

Source: Derived from Table 19.

Conception status apparently operates independently of mother's age to produce variations in infant mortality rates. This is consistent with data on infant mortality by legitimacy status of a birth.

NEONATAL AND POSTNEONATAL MORTALITY

Typically, discussions of infant mortality focus upon the distinction between neonatal infant mortality (deaths during the first month of life) and postneonatal infant mortality (deaths during the second through eleventh month). The distinction is relevant medically since deaths during the first

month of life are generally due to immaturity, congenital malformations and accidents of birth ("endogenous" factors). For
many years the distinction also was thought to be important
socially. It appeared that biological factors were more important
in influencing neonatal mortality than were social factors,
whereas the reverse was true for postneonatal mortality. Recent findings such as the differences in neonatal mortality by
legitimacy status shed doubt on the usefulness of the distinction. Social factors can affect the health of the fetus from the
moment of conception. The health of a child before and after
birth depends upon the medical attention obtained, the mother's diet and general bodily care before birth, and the child's
care after birth, as well as the amount of nurturance and pro-
tective supervision a mother or other adult bestows upon the
child. Among illegitimate children, for example, birth weights
tend to be lower than among legitimate children. Thus prematurity is more common among illegitimate than among
legitimate children [NCHS, 1968:18]. An important consequence of low birth weight and prematurity is a greater than
average risk of infant death [Shapiro et al, 1968:54; Brimblecombe and Ashford, 1968; Richards, 1972].

Of the babies who died at or after their births to the 1966
marriage cohort in California, prematurity was mentioned as a
cause of death of 56 percent of those premaritally conceived
but of only 38 percent of those conceived postmaritally. In
fact, prematurity accounts for 63 percent of the differences in
infant mortality rates between premaritally and postmaritally
conceived babies. If prematurity affected equally children conceived both before and after marriage, than the difference in
infant mortality rates would have been only one-third of the
actual difference observed. The statistical disparity is probably
accounted for by differences in the health of the fetus and of
its mother, for the state of maternal health influences the likelihood of premature birth and of complications consequent to

prematurity. For example, mothers who conceived before marriage were slower to seek prenatal care than were married mothers.

Table 22

INITIATION OF PRENATAL CARE BY CONCEPTION STATUS (IN PERCENT)

Beginning of prenatal care	Premarital N=312	Postmarital N=263
First Trimester	54	68
Second Trimester	32	20
Third Trimester	6	5
No Care	8	7
	100	100
TOTAL	(312)	(263)

Thus far, the analysis has focused on infant mortality by conception status. However, several causes of infant death, including those due to congenital malformations as well as to prematurity, are known to vary according to mother's age [see, e.g., Day, 1967].

INFANT MORTALITY AND MOTHER'S AGE

The California data indicate that mother's age affects infant mortality regardless of conception status, although the relationship is curvilinear. Since most births were to relatively young mothers, and since the actual number of infant deaths was fairly small, the age groupings of mothers had to be large to accommodate statistical analysis. Nonetheless, infant mortality rates were higher for children of older women than for children of teenagers. The gradient of infant mortality associated with rising age of mother is not smooth, however. Children born to mothers aged 15-17 had a greater risk of death than those born to mothers aged 18-19.

Table 23

RATIO OF MORTALITY RATE FOR EACH AGE GROUP TO RATE FOR COMBINED AGES IN EACH LEGITIMACY STATUS GROUP

Age of mother	Premarital conception	Postmarital Conception
15-17	1.07	.89
18-19	.83	.69
20+	1.15	1.28
TOTAL	1.00	1.00

The incidence of deaths associated with prematurity declines by mother's age. Excluding children born between six and one half and eight months after marriage, among whom there might be some question as to the timing of the conception, 51 percent of the deaths to children of mothers aged 15-17 were associated with prematurity. The rate declines to 49 percent for children of mothers aged 20-21, and down to 43 percent for children of mothers aged 22 or older. Whether or not this decline represents a biological or a social phenomenon is still open to question. Following the discussion above with respect to legitimacy status, it has to be noted that the relationship between age of mothers and prematurity could be related to the kind of care a mother receives while pregnant, and thus, the kind of care the fetus receives during gestation. In Table 24 it can be seen that women aged 15-17 initiated prenatal care later than any other age group and had the largest percentages of mothers who received no prenatal care.

The likelihood of specific causes of infant death does not, in most cases, vary substantially from one age group of mothers to the next. The differences that do exist, however, are quite interesting. For example, four children died as a result of maternal toxemia. All four had been born to teenage mothers. Data on maternal mortality indicate that young teenagers and very old women (i.e., those at the two ends of the reproductive continuum) are at greatest risk of toxemia during pregnancy. A final note of interest is the fact that infectious diseases, the major cause of neonatal deaths, are more common among the deaths to children of 15-17 year olds than to older women. This would appear to be a social factor operating in the expected direction.

Table 24
INITIATION OF PRENATAL CARE BY AGE OF MOTHER
(IN PERCENT)

Prenatal Care	Age of Mother			
	15-17	18-19	20-21	22+
First Trimester	45	60	64	72
Second Trimester	36	28	24	18
Third Trimester	9	5	7	2
No Care	10	7	5	8
TOTAL	100	100	100	100
(N)	(152)	(170)	(119)	(134)

PREMATURITY

The sooner after marriage a birth occurs, the higher is the percentage of infant deaths associated with prematurity. This applies to each age group of mothers. This could be construed as an indication that many of the deaths attributed to premarital conceptions were in fact of postmarital conceptions born early, or prematurely, after marriage. Normally, a premature baby is one born between the twenty-eighth and thirty-sixth week after conception or that weighs less than five and one-half pounds at birth. Using the gestational age criterion, however, all births within the first six and one-half months would be too young to be viable, and would normally be abortions or stillbirths, not live births. If there were in fact no relation between prematurity and the timing of a conception before or after marriage, then logically the proportion of infant deaths associated with premature births should not vary from one birth timing to another within each age of mother. If it is true that young mothers have higher proportions of immature children, that proportion should be the same whether a child is born three months or twelve months after marriage.

The data in Table 25 show clearly that the percentage of

Table 25
LOW BIRTH WEIGHT, TIMING OF A BIRTH
AFTER MARRIAGE, AND MOTHER'S AGE

Mother's age at marriage	Months after marriage baby born:							
	0-3		4-6½		6½ - 8		9-24	
	Percent	(N)	Percent	(N)	Percent	(N)	Percent	(N)
15-17	80.4	(46)	58.0	(69)	44.4	(9)	51.4	(37)
18-19	87.5	(24)	59.7	(77)	34.8	(23)	50.7	(69)
20-21	81.3	(16)	66.7	(30)	56.3	(16)	53.4	(73)
22+	94.4	(18)	62.5	(32)	40.0	(15)	53.6	(84)

infant deaths associated with a low birth weight declines dramatically as the interval after marriage increases, regardless of mother's age. Only if all children had been conceived extremely close to the wedding date could the data look like this and not represent differences in the legitimacy status of the conceptions. Even then, it would be difficult to explain how so many babies could be born alive during the first trimester of gestation. The conclusion must be, then, that most of the deaths to children born during the first six and one half months of marriage do, indeed, refer to deaths to premaritally conceived children.

CAUSE OF DEATH

The data generated for this study indicate that infant mortality rates are higher for premaritally conceived than for postmaritally conceived children. Complications arising from prematurity are disproportionately numerous among premaritally conceived children, accounting for much of the difference in infant mortality rates. It is possible to be more specific about which causes of death contribute to differences in infant deaths by conception status. By examining such data, reasonable inferences can be known about differential effects of social factors. In Table 26 are presented cause-specific infant death rates by conception status and mother's age. In all but two instances, death rates are higher for premarital than for postmarital pregnancies regardless of age of mother or cause of infant death. The exceptions are congenital malformations of children of women aged 20-21, and "all other causes" to children of women aged 22 and older.

One of the more interesting aspects of these data is that the pattern of differences is similar for each age of mother. Thus, age of mother does not, per se, help much in accounting for differences in infant death rates by conception status. The reverse is also true. Mother's age and conception status seem to operate somewhat independently of each other.

Overall, we find that exactly 50 percent of the difference in infant mortality rates by conception status is accounted for by the difference in hemolytic diseases of the newborn and other unspecified or ill-defined causes of death that are associated with immaturity. An additional 25 percent of the difference is accounted for by postnatal asphyxia and atelactasis—also frequently associated with immaturity. Only 13 percent of the difference is due to postneonatal infections. None of the difference is due to either congenital malformations, or to accidents, poisoning, and violence.

If we ask why, for example, mothers aged 15-17 have less success keeping their premaritally conceived babies alive than

Table 26

CAUSE-SPECIFIC INFANT DEATH RATES BY MOTHER'S AGE AND PREMARITAL OR POSTMARITAL CONCEPTION STATUS

| | Deaths per 1,000 live births to mothers aged: | | | | | | | |
| | 15-17 | | 18-19 | | 20-21 | | 22+ | |
Cause of death	Pre	Post	Pre	Post	Pre	Post	Pre	Post
Birth injuries	2.0	1.0	2.8	1.1	3.4	2.8	3.5	2.7
Postnatal asphyxia and atelactasis	4.9	2.0	4.3	1.3	4.6	2.1	4.9	1.4
Hemolytic and other diseases of the newborn	10.2	2.7	7.9	2.4	6.9	4.4	13.9	4.1
Congenital malformations	2.2	2.0	2.3	1.3	4.6	4.9	4.2	3.7
Infectious diseases except pneumonia of newborn	6.6	3.4	2.8	2.8	5.1	3.6	6.2	3.3
Total for above five causes	25.9	11.1	20.1	8.9	24.6	17.8	32.7	15.2
Other causes	2.1	1.5	1.5	0.9	1.7	1.1	2.0	2.1
TOTAL	28.0	12.6	21.6	9.8	26.3	18.9	34.7	17.3

mothers aged 18-19, we find that 60 percent of the difference lies in the greater incidence of postneonatal infectious diseases among children of mothers aged 15-17. Among postmaritally conceived children, the difference in infant mortality rates is much less by mother's age, and no single cause of death stands out to account for the observed difference.

NUMERICAL IMPORTANCE OF TEENAGERS

Finally, let us examine the impact of infant deaths to children of teenage mothers on the total number of infant deaths. Of the 638 infant deaths recorded for the live births to the 1966 California marriage cohort, 55 percent were to teenagers. Yet, 62 percent of all first matched births were to teenagers. Thus, the impact of children of teenage mothers on total infant deaths was less than expected. Young teenagers, women aged 15-17 at marriage, however, accounted for 25 percent of all infant deaths and 23 percent of the live births. Within this age group, the level of education about health care, and the financial ability to seek adequate health care, is probably lower than for any other group of women.

In general it seems that the social factors that produce potentially preventable infant deaths tend to operate more within the realm of the teenager than of the older woman. Some live births are potentially viable, but the babies die nonetheless. These situations, evidenced by differences in causes of death, seem to be more frequent among children of teenage mothers than among children of older women.

Having now examined the relationship between teenagers, premarital pregnancies and the problem of infant deaths, we turn in the next chapter to an exploration of the way in which teenage marriages and premarital pregnancies lead to another problem—divorce.

8

MARITAL STABILITY

That teenage marriages are less stable than marriages of older persons is a truism. However, as was discussed in Chapter 1, the marital instability at these ages is largely problematic only if children are involved. A disrupted marriage interferes with the usual socialization and maintenance functions which the family is expected to perform for society. Someone must feed and educate the children, and when a marriage dissolves, this may become more difficult. The presence of children may also help to precipitate a marital dissolution. Christensen, for example, has argued that couples characterized by a premarital pregnancy have the highest divorce rates, followed by couples with early postmarital pregnancies, then by couples whose first birth is conceived well after marriage [Christensen, 1963a: 277].

It also has been noted that marital dissolution may tend to lower fertility since it may interrupt a woman's exposure to the risk of pregnancy [see Davis and Blake, 1956]. However, if the marriages which are dissolved tend to involve young women who have already begun childbearing, then the overall effect of dissolution on subsequent fertility may be less than if childless or older women dominate the divorce statistics.

This is because once her family-building activity has begun, a young woman has less motivation to alter her ideal child-spacing patterns and ideal family size. Couples tend to have preconceived notions about child-spacing and family size, and early marital dissolution will not necessarily affect these values. However, it is known that education and labor force participation have a negative effect on family size, and young childless women are more apt still to be pursuing an education (or at least they have the opportunity to do so) or participating in the labor force than are women with children. Therefore, there is a greater chance that the young childless woman will perceive alternatives to having children.

In childless divorces, dissolution will doubtless delay the onset of reproductive behavior and perhaps lower completed family size. In divorces involving children, dissolution may be only a brief interlude between children. Age is crucial here because the extent to which marriages are generally "youthful" will have an impact on the overall effect on both fertility levels and dissolution rates. The more youthful marriages there are, the higher the dissolution rate is likely to be, and the greater the probable impact of teenage divorces on the population.

HOW MANY TEENAGE MARRIAGES DISSOLVE?

Teenagers have higher divorce rates than couples who are older at marriage, and the dissolution rate has been increasing over time for teenagers, as it has for all ages. Krishnan and Kayami have made estimates of divorce rates in the United States for 1960-1969. Their calculations indicate that divorces climbed steadily through the sixties for every 1,000 married teenage women, from 33 in 1960 to 43 in 1969. Among women aged 20-24, the rates rose from 23 in 1960 to 33 in 1969 [Krishnan and Kayami, 1974:75].

These estimated divorce rates indicate two major empirical

points: teen rates are high; all rates are rising. They do not, however, provide us with estimates of the likelihood of marital failure. Such estimates come primarily from two sources: (1) Census Bureau statistics; and (2) record linkage studies such as the one discussed previously which generated the data for California.

DISSOLUTIONS IN THE UNITED STATES

A nationwide survey conducted by the United States Census Bureau in 1967 revealed that women married between the years 1960-1966, who were less than 18 when they married, had a 2.9 percent chance of a divorce during the first two years of marriage rising to 6.0 percent chance of dissolution during the first five years of marriage.

The 1970 census provided further insights into the marital dissolving habits of teenagers. For example, among women married between 1968 and 1970 who were 14-17 at marriage, almost 9 percent were separated or divorced in April of 1970 when the census was taken. Table 27 indicates that marital

Table 27
WOMEN MARRIED BETWEEN 1968-1970 WHO WERE SEPARATED OR DIVORCED IN 1970: UNITED STATES (IN PERCENT)

Age at first marriage	Separated or divorced
14-17	8.7
18-19	4.9
20-24	3.3
25-29	3.8
30+	5.2

Source: United States Bureau of the Census (1973:Table 4).

stability increases with age at marriage up through ages 20-24, after which it starts to decline. In a majority of cases, the couples are separated rather than divorced, indicating that the incidence of divorce is only a minimum estimate of marital instability.

In recent years marital instability has not changed much. Among women married in 1965-1967 who were 14-17 at marriage, 13 percent were separated or divorced by 1970, and among those married in 1960-64, also 13 percent were separated or divorced in 1970. Among women married at ages 18-19 in 1960-1964 and 1965-1967, the incidence of separation and divorce was 10 percent after the first five through ten years after marriage. The same differences in marital stability by age at marriage exist for males as for females. In the United States, then, teenage marriages do have a higher probability of ending in separation or divorce than do marriages of older persons. Furthermore, young teenage brides or grooms (ages 14-17) are more likely to have a marriage dissolved than older teenagers (ages 18-19).

Data from the census survey of 1967 also show that early marital dissolutions are less frequent among childless couples than among couples with children, regardless of the age of the bride. This is interesting because it suggests that children are a destabilizing influence, at least early in marriage, even though the American normative system has leaned toward the maintenance of an unsatisfactory marriage if children are involved. Yet, greater stability among childless couples would seem to be consistent with a recent study conducted by the Institute of Social Research at the University of Michigan. In a sample of 2,000 American women, this study found that 72 percent of the childless couples between the ages of 18 and 29 described themselves as happy, compared to 65 percent of the couples who had a child under six years of age in the house [Institute for Social Research, 1974:4].

It is possible that children per se are not detrimental to a marriage, but rather that children resulting from premarital pregnancies, who had forced an unwanted marriage, are less of a cohesive force than children conceived postmaritally. The data generated for the marriage cohort of 1966 in California seem to follow this same pattern as I shall discuss below.

DISSOLUTION IN CALIFORNIA

Before analyzing the dissolution data for California which were generated by the linkage of vital records, it is important to make a few notes regarding the nature of these data and their inherent limitations.

In the course of the record linkage, the first preliminary report filed by a couple seeking to obtain a marital dissolution was matched with the couple's marriage record. Since frequently there were multiple types of dissolution (e.g., divorce in combination with separation) indicated on the preliminary report, for analytical purposes, all types have been lumped into a single category of marital dissolution. The term "marital dissolution" is a bit misleading, however, because no data were available on the actual outcome of the dissolution action. The action could have been dropped and the couples reconciled; it could have been granted as requested; or it could have been (in a small percentage of cases) denied. The data as generated here reflect an index of marital instability which has been formally recognized by one or both of the marriage partners. This information is reported by the spouse initiating the preliminary dissolution complaint. The pattern that emerges in California is similar, but not identical, to the pattern for the United States. During the first three years of marriage, the probability of a marriage breaking up was highest for women married at ages 15 and 16. Among these women, almost a fourth of all marriages were dissolving after three years (see Figure 10). As the age at marriage goes up after age 16, the likelihood of dissolution goes down consistently. Among 19 year-old brides, 14 percent of the marriages had dissolved by the end of three years.

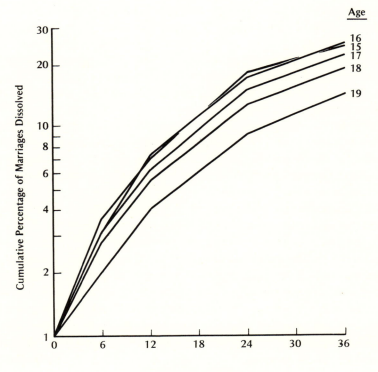

Figure 10
MARITAL INSTABILITY BY AGE AT MARRIAGE
CALIFORNIA MARRIAGE COHORT, 1966

MARITAL STABILITY AND CHILDBEARING IN CALIFORNIA

A rather complex relationship between childbearing and marital instability exists in California. It is generally true that childless women are less likely to be separated from their husbands than are women with children, but the impact of children is different at different ages. In Table 28 it can be seen that at ages 15 and 16, women with postmarital pregnancies are slightly more likely to have an unstable marriage than women with a premarital pregnancy, and both groups have more unstable marriages than do childless women.

Among 17 and 18 year old brides, Christensen's thesis is confirmed that marital instability is greatest for premarital conceivers, followed by postmarital conceivers, and finally by childless women. Among women aged 19 and older when they were married, the postmarital conceivers have slightly lower rates of instability than do childless women, although the differences are not large.

These data lead clearly to the speculation that at the young teen ages, the arrival of a child early in marriage, whether conceived before or after marriage, is a destabilizing influence. For women aged 19 and older, the arrival of a postmaritally conceived child is a stabilizing influence (i.e., apparently a "wanted" child) whereas a premaritally conceived child is a relatively destabilizing influence. Yet age alone seems to increase the ability or desire of couples to keep a marriage intact despite the timing of a child in marriage. These conclusions are clearly at variance with the thesis advanced by Winch [1962:602] that the correlation between marital instability and age at marriage would disappear if allowances could be made for premarital pregnancies.

Another important aspect of the relationship between childbearing and marital instability is the fact that youthful marital dissolutions are far more likely to involve children, especially premaritally conceived children, than are dissolutions involving older brides. For example, among 15 year old brides, 59

Table 28

SEPARATIONS DURING THE FIRST 36 MONTHS AFTER MARRIAGE
BY CHILDBEARING STATUS ACCORDING TO BRIDE'S AGE AT FIRST MARRIAGE:
CALIFORNIA MARRIAGE COHORT, 1966

Separated couples had first birth within:	Age at first marriage								
	15	16	17	18	19	20	21	22-24	25-44
0-8 months									
Number separated	112	468	644	724	463	184	102	125	69
Women at risk	433	1,713	2,616	3,357	2,606	1,395	906	1,306	676
Percent separated	25.9	27.3	24.6	21.5	17.8	13.2	11.3	9.6	10.2
8-24 months									
Number separated	32	192	277	501	316	148	93	114	71
Women at risk	90	633	1,292	2,749	2,609	1,698	1,306	2,223	1,582
Percent separated	35.6	30.3	21.4	18.2	12.1	8.8	7.1	5.1	4.5
No births, 0-24 months									
Number separated	47	362	675	1,596	1,346	681	571	878	707
Women at risk	289	1,993	3,901	9,270	10,704	7,688	6,791	11,994	8,822
Percent separated	16.3	18.2	17.3	17.2	12.5	8.9	8.4	7.3	8.0

percent of the dissolutions occurring during the first three years of marriage involve a child conceived premaritally, whereas at ages 25-44, only 8 percent of dissolutions involve a premaritally conceived child (see Table 29).

Thus far the discussion has focused on all separations occurring during the first 36 months after marriage. Does age at marriage and pregnancy status also affect the timing of a marital break-up?

Table 29

SEPARATIONS DURING THE FIRST 36 MONTHS OF MARRIAGE ACCORDING TO BRIDE'S AGE AT MARRIAGE: CALIFORNIA MARRIAGE COHORT, 1966

Age at first marriage	Percentage of separations associated with:			
	A birth 0-8 mos.	A birth 8-24 mos.	No birth	N
15	59	17	24	191
16	46	19	35	1,022
17	41	17	42	1,596
18	26	18	56	2,821
19	22	15	63	2,125
20	18	15	67	1,013
21	13	12	75	766
22-24	11	10	79	1,117
25-44	8	8	83	847

HOW SOON DO TEENAGE MARRIAGES DISSOLVE?

The data for California suggest that the timing of a marital separation early in a teenage marriage is related to the timing of a child early in marriage (Table 30). Among women who separate from their husbands during the first three years of marriage, those without children are on average the quickest to dissolve the marriage. There are few differences by age in this respect, save for the fact that 15 year olds are the earliest marital dissolvers. Since the number of dissolutions to 15 year

Table 30

**CUMULATIVE DISTRIBUTION OF SEPARATIONS TO WOMEN
DURING THE FIRST TWO YEARS OF MARRIAGE,
BY AGE AT FIRST MARRIAGE AND TIMING OF FIRST BIRTH:
CALIFORNIA, 1966**

Age at first marriage and months to first birth	Months from marriage to separation				
	6	12	24	36	N
0-8 mos.					
15	13	29	78	100	112
16	8	27	70	100	468
17	10	26	68	100	644
18	14	32	74	100	670
19	12	29	64	100	463
20-44	13	31	69	100	477
8-24 mos.					
15	19	28	66	100	32
16	14	30	69	100	192
17	15	23	61	100	277
18	13	26	60	100	501
19	11	25	58	100	316
20-44	14	28	65	100	426
Childless women					
15	28	47	83	100	47
16	25	42	77	100	362
17	26	43	77	100	675
18	21	38	72	100	1,496
19	19	37	71	100	1,346
20-44	22	40	72	100	2,957

olds is small, however, annulments probably account for almost all of the childless marital breakups. At each age, nearly a fourth of all separations to childless women occurred during the first six months of marriage.

Women whose first child was born within the first eight months of marriage tend to be next in order of early timing of dissolution, followed closely by those women who bore a child during the eighth through the twenty-fourth months of marriage. Again, there were few differences by age in the timing of dissolutions.

INSTABILITY AND GROOM'S AGE

In Chapter 4, it was noted that premarital pregnancies seemed to be related to the relative ages of bride and groom. It is not unreasonable to suppose that the incidence of marital instabil-

Table 31

INCIDENCE OF MARITAL SEPARATION DURING FIRST
THREE YEARS OF MARRIAGE BY TIMING OF FIRST CHILD
ACCORDING TO RELATIVE AGE OF GROOM,
FOR BRIDES AGES 15-19:
CALIFORNIA, 1966

Conception of first birth	Younger		Same		Older	
	Percent	N	Percent	N	Percent	N
Early premarital	22.0	440	19.6	1,420	21.2	6,923
Late premarital	16.7	168	22.3	641	19.9	3,432
Postmarital	15.8	298	15.7	1,170	15.0	8,503
No child	19.4	640	15.8	3,257	15.3	24,325
TOTAL	19.1	1,546	17.2	6,488	16.6	43,181

ity would also be similarly related. One might well reason that an older male would be more likely to introduce stability into a marriage with a teenage girl than would a groom younger than the bride.

The data for California suggest, however, that few significant differences exist in the incidence of dissolution among 15-19 year old brides according to the relative age of the groom. These data are shown in Table 31. The only difference which might be significant is for childless couples, for whom it appears that, indeed, grooms older than brides were associated with lower incidences of dissolution than grooms younger than their brides.

INSTABILITY BY RACE AND ETHNICITY

In California it appears that marital dissolution is more common among white than among nonwhite teenagers. However, at ages over 19 there is practically no difference by race. The differences are greatest for teenagers who conceived a child premaritally. Among such women, the dissolution rates among whites is almost 50 percent higher than among nonwhites. These data are shown in Table 32.

Almost exactly the same comments can be made with respect to Mexican-American ethnicity. Non-Mexican-American teenagers have higher rates of dissolution than do Mexican-American teenagers, and virtually no differences exist at the older ages (see Table 33). However, among teenagers, the ethnic difference in dissolution widens as the timing of a child after marriage increases. The differences are least among early premarital conceivers and greatest among the childless couples. These ethnic differentials in divorce seem to be at variance with the usual explanations of why teenage marriages are less stable than other marriages.

Table 32

SEPARATION RATES FOR WHITES AND NONWHITES, BY AGE AT MARRIAGE AND TIMING OF
FIRST BIRTH: CALIFORNIA, 1966

	White			Nonwhite		
	Total marriages	Number of separations	Percent of separations	Total marriages	Number of separations	Percent of separations
Early premarital						
15-19	7,450	1,633	21.9	1,333	198	14.9
20+	2,577	283	11.0	611	62	10.1
Late premarital						
15-19	3,939	796	20.2	302	55	18.2
20+	1,689	170	10.1	264	18	6.8
Postmarital						
15-19	9,154	1,382	15.1	834	114	13.7
20+	7,649	421	5.5	1,074	72	6.7
Childless						
15-19	26,544	4,075	15.4	2,170	258	11.9
20+	36,162	2,894	8.0	4,372	351	8.0
TOTAL						
15-19	47,087	7,886	16.7	4,639	625	13.4
20+	48,077	3,768	7.8	6,321	503	8.0

Table 33
SEPARATION RATES BY SPANISH-SURNAME
ACCORDING TO AGE AT MARRIAGE AND TIMING OF FIRST BIRTH
CALIFORNIA MARRIAGE COHORT 1966

| | Spanish Surname ? | | | | | |
| | Yes | | | No | | |
	Total marriages	(N) Separations	(percent) Separations	Total marriages	(N) Separations	(percent) Separations
Early premarital						
15-19	1,862	320	17.2	6,990	1,582	22.6
20+	796	71	8.9	2,392	274	11.5
Late premarital						
15-19	597	93	15.6	3,657	758	20.7
20+	303	27	8.9	1,649	161	9.8
Postmarital						
15-19	2,017	234	11.6	7,954	1,262	15.9
20+	2,032	114	5.6	6,690	378	5.7
Childless						
15-19	3,290	366	11.1	25,498	3,967	15.6
20+	5,137	436	8.5	36,043	2,809	7.8
TOTAL						
15-19	7,766	1,013	13.0	44,099	7,569	17.2
20+	8,268	648	7.8	46,774	3,622	7.7

WHY DO TEENAGE MARRIAGES DISSOLVE?

Much has been said in the literature about the possible reasons for the higher incidence of dissolution among teenage marriages than among marriages of older people. Most of the reasons seem to boil down to economic instability. Burchinal [1965] claims that persons involved in young marriages typically have lower educational levels, lower IQs, and lower socioeconomic status than comparable groups of unmarrieds. They thus are characterized by economic instability, which often has been implicated as a divorce-producing factor. Economic instability may also underlie the higher than average dissolution rates frequently noted for the lower social classes. Social class also tends to confound the relationships among age, fertility, and dissolution. Bartz and Nye [1970] note that the lower the social class, the more likely will heterosexual involvement begin at an early age. Following that logic, it would also seem that an earlier onset of sexual activity among the lower classes would lead to higher incidences of early pregnancy, and thus to a potentially unstable marriage. Most of this logic is voided, however, by Kantner and Zelnick's [1972b] finding that there are, in fact, few actual class differences in the onset of sexual activity (discussed above in Chapter 4).

Coombs and Freedman [1970] found that among a sample of white couples in Detroit followed from 1961-1966, a premaritally conceived child appeared to produce a lasting economic disadvantage over couples who conceived their first child after marriage. The thesis of economic instability leading to dissolution fits the California data to the extent that California marriages of pregnant brides were less stable than of those who became pregnant postmaritally, and youthful marriages are less stable than marriages of older persons. However, the California data indicate that teenage marriages among racial and ethnic minorities tend to be more stable than those in the dominant Anglo population. If racial and ethnic minority status is accompanied by greater economic instability than is true for Anglos, then we should find that teenage marital instability is greater, not less, in the minority groups than in the Anglo population. The inference is that the economic argument is not wholly adequate. Among nonwhites, it is known that the incidence of illegitimacy and of keeping an illegitimate child is higher than among whites. This suggests that forced marriages are perhaps less likely to occur among nonwhites than whites, and marital stability may be a bit higher. Among Mexican-Americans, the influence of Catholicism may operate to lower the likelihood of a formal reporting of marital problems by filing for a divorce. Thus, it may be that among nonwhites, many potentially unstable marriages are never formally contracted, whereas among Mexican-Americans, dissolutions of such marriages are not reported. The reality may thus be that fewer racial or ethnic differences actually exist in the incidence of instability among teenage parents than has been heretofore believed.

REMARRIAGES AMONG TEENAGERS

Since dissolution rates are higher for women married as teenagers than they are for women married when older, it is reasonable to expect that remarriages will occur more frequently among women who were in their teens when they married for the first time. Data from the 1970 census support this reasoning. Among all women who dissolve their first marriage, teenage brides exhibit a greater tendency to remarry than do divorced women who were older brides. These data, shown in Table 34, indicate, for example, that among women first married between 1960 and 1964 and subsequently divorced, 73 percent of those who had been 14-17, but only 54 percent of those who had been 20 or older, had remarried by 1970. The same pattern holds for first marriages contracted in 1965-1967.

The relationship does not hold for marriages in the period 1968-1970, but marriages would have been of such short duration at that point that little emphasis should be placed on remarriage rates during that period. One implication of these data is that many teenage marriages might indeed be trial marriages, with the dissolving partners (at least females) remarrying in high proportion after the first marriage failed to work out.

The number of women who remarry while still a teenager is fairly small, but data for California suggest that among those who do, the rates of premarital and postmarital pregnancy are far less than among the first-time brides. From age 17 on up, there is a general decline in the incidence of premarital pregnancy among previously married women. Compared to women in first marriages it can be observed that premarital pregnancy among 17 year old remarrying brides is only 40 percent as likely as among first-time brides. Postmarital pregnancies are also far less frequent among previously married brides than

Table 34

**REMARRIAGE RATES AMONG WOMEN WHOSE FIRST MARRIAGE
ENDED IN DIVORCE: UNITED STATES 1970
(IN PERCENT)**

Age at first marriage	Remarried: first marriage ocurring in:[a]		
	1968-1970	1965-1967	1960-1964
14-17	34.6	55.2	73.0
18-19	25.1	48.0	66.4
20+	33.4	43.3	54.4

Source: United States Bureau of the Census, 1973, Table 4.

[a]Calculated as the number of women married more than once after the first marriage ended in divorce/women divorced and remarried + women divorced and not remarried.

among first-time brides. Teenagers accounted for only 3.5 percent of remarrying brides in 1966, yet accounted for 16.4 percent of premarital pregnancies and 11.8 percent of postmarital pregnancies to remarrying women. The generally very low incidence of pregnancy among previously married brides suggests considerable contraceptive effectiveness among such women. It is probable that her prior marital experience enhanced her knowledge and practice of contraception.

In conclusion, it should be noted that although teenage marriages are more likely to dissolve than are marriages of older persons, a majority of teenage marriages remain intact over time. This is one perspective on teenage marriages that will be examined in Chapter 9.

9

TEENAGE MARRIAGES IN PERSPECTIVE

Teenage marriages represent a problem to American society. They are disproportionately associated with illegitimate conceptions and with marital instability. These are not mutually exclusive problems, but rather tend to interact with each other and with still other problems: illegitimate conceptions are disproportionately associated with infant deaths; a premaritally conceived birth contributes to rapid early marital childbearing activity; and the children, in turn, contribute to marital instability.

It is probable, of course, that as long as there is premarital sexual intercourse, there will be illegitimate conceptions, especially among novice teenagers. It is also probable that as long as there is an institution of marriage, some of the illegitimate conceptions will be legitimized by marriage. A situation of perfect contraceptive utilization (including use of sterilization and abortion) is an unrealizable utopia. Even in a society with perfect birth prevention knowledge and technology, you may still find women who feel compelled to use pregnancy as a stepping stone to adulthood or to marriage. Furthermore, as long as teenagers live in a social world which perceives them as adolescents or as youths rather than as adults, the quest for adult-

hood through marriage or childbearing may remain fairly prev-
alent, and the frustrations inherent in a marriage with small
children and probable low financial resources will continue to
take their toll in terms of infant health and marital instability.
Nonetheless, these comments should not be taken to mean that
the fairly high levels of teenage marriage and fertility in the
United States are standard demographic phenomena.

CROSS-CULTURAL COMPARISON OF TEENAGE MARRIAGE AND FERTILITY

In California in 1970, 12 percent of all teenage women had
been married at least once. This is a rather high percentage by
the standards of the industrialized world. Nowhere in Western
Europe and Asia are countries found with more than 8 percent
of its teenagers married. The California data are comparable to
so-called "second-world" nations in Eastern Europe and in
South America. Only in Africa, the Middle East, and Southeast
Asia do higher percentages of married teenagers prevail. Perhaps
more than any other industrialized nation, the United States
has chosen an anti-Malthusian approach to low fertility. We are
a nation of youthful marriages in which all faith for a low
birthrate is placed on contraceptive use, rather than relying on
the Malthusian prescription of delayed marriage, and continence
before marriage, to keep the birthrate in check.

Accompanying higher-than-average percentages of teenage
women who are married is a higher-than-average birth rate
among teenagers. In 1966 in California, there were 81 births
per 1,000 teenagers. In 1973 that rate had declined substantially to 48 births per 1,000 teenage women, as was discussed in
Chapter 3. Nevertheless, the California teenage birthrate is still
higher than in Western European or Asian countries. It is lower
than in Africa, the Middle East, or Southeast Asia, but about
in line with countries in Eastern Europe and South America.

Where teenage marriage is fairly common, the teenage birth

rate tends to be high. For most countries, this means that teen-age fertility has a higher-than-average impact on the overall level of fertility. For example, in both the United States as a whole and in California in 1968, 17 percent of all births were to teenagers. This was more than for most countries for which data are available according to statistics published in the United Nations Demographic Yearbook [1973b] . Only two countries, Camaroon (1965) and Barbados (1969) had significantly high-er percentages, with 26 and 24 percent, respectively. Other countries which in the 1960s experienced a teenage impact on total fertility similar to the level for the United States include Pakistan (16 percent in 1965), Venezuela (15 percent in 1968), Guatemala (17 percent in 1969), Honduras (17 percent in 1968), Puerto Rico (16 percent in 1970), El Salvador (17 per-cent in 1970), Panama (18 percent in 1970), Liberia (19 per-cent in 1970), and Bulgaria (17 percent in 1970).

It appears, then, that the highly industrialized United States is comparable to many, and is exceeded by few, underdeveloped nations in terms of the influence that teenagers have on mar-riage and fertility. An important difference appears, however. The completed family size in the United States is smaller than in most of these other countries. Americans are generally in a position to have their cake and eat it too with respect to de-cision-making about marriage and childbearing. In the United States today most, although certainly not all, couples have the social and economic freedom to marry when they want to and to have as many or as few children as they wish. Most people are in a position to make rational cost-benefit estimates of mar-riage and reproduction, even if they do not go through such a process at a conscious level. For example, the standard of liv-ing began to decline in the United States in real dollars in 1969, and this probably helped to account for the decline in early marriage. The flexibility of young couples is apparent in their ability to respond quickly to such an economic stimulus by lowering marriage and fertility rates (see Chapters 2 and 3).

One of the things that we really do not know, however, is the age at which people actually do make those kinds of calculations.

GAPS IN CURRENT KNOWLEDGE

We are only beginning to arrive at a good understanding of why teenagers in the United States marry and have children as they do, and there is still a great deal we do not know. How many of the 15 or 16 year old brides were behaving in a way consistent with a rational conception of their life-chances, and how many were victims of social situational circumstances, pressured into marriage or a child that they did not want? Among brides in California in 1966, 81 percent of all 15 year olds bore a child within the first two years of marriage, compared to 39 percent of the 19 year olds and 18 percent of the 22-24 year olds. Was each age group of brides operating rationally within different paradigms of social reality? Or were the younger women victims of poor education and peer or parental pressure to a greater (or lesser) extent than the older brides? These are questions that await answers.

Figure 11 illustrates the various paths by which a teenager might arrive at a married status. The task of further research will be to decipher the social mechanisms which are represented in the diagram by the arrows linking each pair of social situations. The diagram represents the possible combinations of premarital sexual activity and of contraceptive and abortion utilization which are open to a woman regardless of age. All of the explanations for the rise since World War II in illegitimacy and premarital conceptions can be found within this diagram. For example, Davis [1973] has summarized the causes of the increase in unmarried reproduction as being (a) the rise in the prevalence and promiscuity of premarital intercourse, which is subsumed under division I in Figure 11; (b) an increased ability to cure venereal disease before it causes sterility, subsumed under division III, or spontaneous abortion, subsumed under division IV; (c) a tendency from the 1930s to the 1960s toward more rigorous enforcement of the anti-abortion laws, subsumed under division IV; (d) a tendency for the family planning movement to shift the burden of contraception onto the female, subsumed under division II; (e) a growing disposition to free the male from responsibility for illegitimate reproduction, subsumed under division V; (f) a tendency for illegitimate motherhood to be subsidized by the government, which in tan-

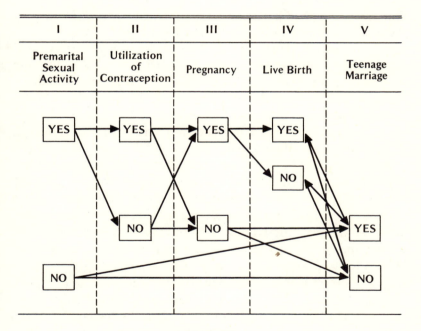

Figure 11
THE STRUCTURE OF PREMARITAL SEXUAL ACTIVITY,
PREGNANCY, AND MARRIAGE

dem with (e) makes nonmarriage easier, subsumed under division V; and (g) "a relaxation of adult supervision over premarital relationships and mate selection which has thrown women into a ruthless competitive struggle for husbands," [Davis, 1973:251], and proceeds to elaborate on the theme that premarital pregnancies are a result of a conscious desire on the part of the girl to entrap the man, or of the nonuse or careless use of contraceptives, or the nonavailability or nonuse of abortions.

Of course, we must be careful, when examining teenage marriages generally, to make a distinction first between a teenage woman who marries when she is pregnant, and one who marries without the complication of an existing or impending child. One, we know, had participated in premarital sexual activity. We would also like to know, then, what motivated the girl to engage in sexual relations in the first place, why she (or her male partner) failed to use a contraceptive (or failed to use one effectively), and why she failed to seek an abortion, as well. We then would like to know what motivated her and her partner to decide to marry, and what factors determined particular timing of the marriage in relation to the birth of a child. For the teenage girl who married without the burden of pregnancy, we would like to know first whether a false pregnancy or an aborted pregnancy (spontaneous or induced) precipitated the marriage, but did not result in a birth. For the women who have no pregnancy history at all, we would like to know both whether and why they did or did not engage in sexual activity. If they did participate in premarital sexual activity, we would then want to know whether they utilized contraceptives, or engaged in coitus less often than women who became pregnant, or were simply "lucky" (in which case most demographers would likely label them as being less fecund than the teenage brides). Further, we would want to know why teenage women who were not pregnant would be motivated to marry.

At this juncture we are primarily aided in our ability to

judge the future course of events in teenage marriages by inferences that we can draw about probable demographic and social
influences. We don't yet know enough about specific motiva-
tions for teenagers to marry to be able to say that if motivation X in the social structure were changed, then teenage marriages would be reduced by x percent. The problem lies in the
fact that motives and causes are not synonymous. The cause
of a pregnancy is unprotected sexual intercourse, regardless of
the motives of the sexual partners. Indeed, Kantner and Zelnick's 1971 survey of teenagers showed that of those women
who had not been protected against pregnancy during their
last intercourse, only 16 percent gave "a desire to be pregnant"
as their reason for not having used a contraceptive. On the other hand, the nonavailability of contraception in that situation
was given as a reason by 30 percent of the nonusers [Shah,
Zelnick and Kantner, 1975].

Once pregnant, there may be several possible explanations
(i.e., causes) for a woman not to seek an abortion (such as
embarrassment, parental pressure, fear of complications, or
excessive cost), regardless of her motives. Motives are difficult
to measure and thus we have only a limited knowledge of them.
However, influences such as the changes in the age structure,
and the provision of birth prevention measures to teenagers
are relatively easy to measure, they therefore receive much
more attention.

TEENAGE MARRIAGES AND THE AGE STRUCTURE

The decline in fertility rates in this country since 1957 has
resulted in successively smaller cohorts which, through an age
effect alone, could reduce the impact of teenage marriage and
fertility in the United States. In 1966 in the United States,
teenagers represented 22 percent of all women in the reproductive ages of 15-44. By 1981, teenagers will represent only 18
percent of all women aged 15-44—an 18 percent decline. Even

more significantly, in 1966 there were 20 percent *more* wom-
en in the United States who were aged 15-19 than there were
women aged 20-24. By 1981, there will be 7 percent *fewer.*
These changes in the age structure alone will tend to lower
significantly the impact that teenagers have on national levels
of marriage and fertility, even though they may not change
the rates themselves.

In the California marriage cohort of 1966, teenagers represented 48 percent of all first-time brides. By 1973, teenagers
represented only 38 percent of all first-time California brides.
In Chapter 2 I discussed the fact that this decline is due entirely to a substantial decrease in the probability of a girl getting
married before age 20. These changes were taking place at a
time when the baby-boom women were moving into marriageable ages, and so actually we should have expected an increase
in the proportion of brides who are teenagers. Thus, during
the late sixties and early seventies there were obviously changes
occurring in the rate at which teenagers married. What we do
not yet know is the extent to which these changes reflect changes in motivation and to what extent they reflect changes in the
means available to postpone marriage. One such means is the
availability of birth prevention measures.

TEENAGE BIRTH PREVENTION

Changes in the normative structure which permit the provision of contraceptive and abortion services to teenagers, as
well as expanded programs of sex and birth control education,
should in the future help to ease the problem of unwanted
teenage fertility, thus eliminating some of the teenage marriages. Data from the 1970 National Fertility Study indicate
that during the mid-1960s an increasing proportion of women
began using contraception before marriage [Rindfuss and
Westoff, 1974:79]. The increase was experienced by younger

and older women alike and appears to be directly related
to the introduction of oral contraceptives. Yet, in many
cities in the United States teenagers continue to be educated
about their reproductive system, and especially about birth
control techniques primarily on "the street" rather than in
school.

It should also be reemphasized that future levels of unwanted
teenage fertility, whether within marriage or not, depend much
more heavily upon the birth preventive motivation of women
than of men [Davis, 1973]. The equality of the sexes as well
as the female-oriented direction of the family planning movement and of welfare services, all place the onus of responsibility
for preventing a birth much more on the woman involved than
on the man. At least some portion of teenage fertility is not
wanted, and is occasioned by ignorance or by the momentary
lack of contraceptives or by the lack of willingness to seek an
abortion. Thus, it is likely that as information and services are
disseminated more widely among teenagers, the percentage of
brides who are pregnant at each age may diminish, even if the
pattern of an inverse relationship between age at marriage and
the incidence of premarital pregnancy continues.

The impact upon American society of the problems associated with teenage marriages should abate in proportion to the
probable decline in the incidence of teenage marriages and fertility. Yet, only when we have the whys linked up between each
pair of boxes in Figure 11—only when we know specifically
why some teenagers marry and others do not—will we be fully
able to propose pragmatic answers to the problems created
for society by teenagers who marry.

Appendix A

TECHNICAL DISCUSSION OF RECORD LINKAGES

The data generated for this study were produced by a record linkage of marriage, birth, and divorce records for the State of California. The record linkage system used in this study was a refinement of a system developed earlier and reported by Weeks [1972]. Since the linkage of dissolution data with marriage records was accomplished primarily through an adaptation of the original system, whereas the marriage and birth linkage was accomplished via the refined method, both systems will be discussed.

METHODOLOGY IN FIRST STUDY

The objective of the record linkage in that first study was to match the marriages occurring in 1966 in California among never-previously married women with the births to those women in California in 1965-1969, and with the preliminary findings for dissolution occurring in California in 1966-1969. Since all records were on computer tape, the linkage itself was carried out via a computerized process, although records were inspected visually when desirable.

The method used to link records was an adaptation of that

developed by Kennedy, Newcombe, and others [1965]. I will discuss here only the marriage and births match. The marriage and identification were common to the marriage and birth records in California, and had been coded onto computer tape:

Birth Records	Marriage Records
Child's surname	Groom's surname
Father's first initial	Groom's first initial
Father's middle initial	Groom's middle initial
Mother's maiden surname	Bride's maiden surname
Mother's age	Bride's age
County of occurrence	County of occurrence

The first five letters of the male surname and the first three letters of the female maiden surname were used as sorting and screening variables. In other words, a match of records was attempted only if the abbreviated surnames agreed completely on the marriage and birth records. Once a set of marriage records with identical abbreviated surnames was brought together with a set of birth records with the same surname combinations, the decision had to be made as to which marriage records (if any) matched with which birth records.

At first glance, the extent of agreement could be appropriately determined simply by seeing how many of the variables common to both records were in fact the same. Such a system implicitly assigned a positive weight to an agreement of variables and a negative weight to nonagreements. The sum of these weights thus influenced the decision to accept or reject a match. The problem of how much weight to attach to an agreement or disagreement of variables, although not handled easily by intuition, was amenable to quantification. A human filing clerk matching by hand typically makes subjective judgments which have a quantitative element but which typically suffer from their lack of consistency. The task of the programmer is to make precise the rules which can be applied for deciding whether two pieces of information both refer to the same individual.

Newcombe [1965a] developed a set of procedures to be used for determining weights assigned to an agreement or disagreement of common items of identification. The weight which Newcombe suggests might reasonably be assigned to a match is a number proportional to the probability that this match has occurred other than by chance. The information necessary to calculate these probabilities is contained within the files themselves, but human subjectivity is involved. Essentially we want to know the relative frequencies of matches of our secondary matching variables among those records which are judged to be actual matches as opposed to those matches which occur in randomly selected pairs of records. The judgment of actual record matching is initially made by subjecting several hundred records to hand matching and by using the intuition—which we ultimately want to avoid—to help develop matching and nonmatching frequencies for the secondary matching variables.

The numerical determination of the weights involves performing matches by hand, creating in the process two sets of records: those which are genuinely linked, and those which are fortuitously brought together because of surname-code similarities. Since more information is available on each record than is coded onto tape, visual scrutiny appears to be nearly perfect. Agreement among secondary matching variables (non-screening variables) is more common among the genuinely linked pairs, and the ratio of frequencies of agreements (or disagreements) between linked and unlinked pairs can indicate the magnitude of the odds for or against a true match. Thus for each variable agreement or disagreement a weight was assigned on the following basis: If, on a pair of records brought together for matching, secondary variable x_i on records from file (1) agreed with secondary variable x_i on records from file (2), then a positive weight was assigned to that agreement. The weights were derived as follows:

$$\text{Weight for agreement} = \log_2(a/b)$$

where a = frequency of agreement of variable x_i on pairs of linked records

b = frequency of agreement of variable x_i on pairs of unlinked records.

If variables $x_{i(1)}$ and $x_{i(2)}$ did not match, then a negative weight was assigned which was the inverse of the positive weight. When all variables had been checked for agreement or disagreement and the appropriate weights assigned to each agreement or disagreement, the weights were summed and the determination made on the basis of that sum as to whether or not the two records did in fact match. The evaluation of the weights was based on the experience derived from hand matching.

The weights permitted a numerical interpretation of the probability that a match had occurred other than by chance. Initially the weights were derived from a preliminary hand matching of 100 marriage records and approximately 250 birth records. Hand matching was necessary at first to determine precisely which records matched and which did not. Armed with the derived weights, it was then possible to go back and determine numerically which weight sums represented true matches, false matches or questionable cases. With a numerical test for rejection or acceptance added to the procedure, a larger proportion of the file could be checked on the computer to verify or update matching and nonmatching frequencies derived from hand matching.

The weights derived from hand matching indicated initially that the middle initial of the male, with a weight of 4, was the best discriminator of matching and nonmatching records, followed by female age, with a weight of 3. Using these weights, it was possible to run through the entire marriage file looking for birth matches with a clearer idea of what might or might not constitute a match. In this way, all possible variable comparisons were checked. The principal difference between the hand matching results and the computerized entire-file results was the change in rank order of the male first initial. Male first initial emerged as the best indicator of a match with a weight of 4, followed by male middle initial and female age, both with weights of 3.

There are at least two ways of handling the weighting procedure. The first would be to compare variable x_i on records for files A and B, and if agreement exists, add the appropriate weight to the total sum. If no agreement exists, then subtract the nonmatching weight from total weight sum. A second way of proceeding is simply to add weight if there is agreement, and neither add nor subtract anything if there is disagreement. The second procedure was followed for the marriage and birth linkage, with a replication for one year being done using the first method as a check on the consistency of the two procedures. The second procedure was also used throughout for the marriage and divorce linkages.

The advantage of adding only positive weight and never accounting for negative weight is that it reduces the fuzziness of the marginal matches. For example, it was found that when using the first method whereby weights are added for agreement and subtracted for disagreement, some total weights which always constituted a match were lower than some weights which represented a mixture of positive and false matches. This problem arose because some combinations of matching variables indicated a greater likelihood of a match than did other combinations. In other words, the matching variables were not completely independent of cross correlation with each other although independence of correlation is a major assumption of the weighting procedure. Utilizing positive weights only cannot eliminate the above type of inconsistencies, but it does reduce them, thereby making easier the checking of marginal or tentative matches.

It should be noted that complete agreement was not required on all variables to establish a positive weight. For example, in comparing the remainder of a surname (either male or female), of that portion not used in the searching process, two letters were allowed to be in disagreement as an allowance principally for misspelling. Similarly, in the case of age, since the actual birthdate was not available to work with, a sufficient range had to be allowed so that change in age between two time periods could have been within the range of probability, given the uncertainty of actual birth dates. However, with respect to place of occurrence I did make an allowance for differential probabilities of matching. If the place-of-occurrence matched on any county other than Los Angeles County (code '70'), I arbitrarily raised the weight attached to such a match from +2 to +3 since Los Angeles County is the largest in the state and thus has the greatest likelihood of occurring on either a valid matching pair or a nonmatching pair of records.

On the basis of the sum of the individual weights, decisions were made about further processing of the match. Prior to any evaluation of the weights, however, the match was assessed according to the agreement of the full surnames. Since considerable leeway was given in the comparison test for error, no more tolerance was felt desirable. Therefore, regardless of total weight, any match in which either the full female or male surname did not agree within two-character tolerance limits was rejected. If the match survived the name-test and the weights added to twelve or more, a match was assumed unless another birth record (of the same birth order) matched the same marriage record, but with a higher weight.

If the total test-weight was less than seven, the match was rejected without further ado. If the match survived the name test and the total sum of weights was less than twelve but greater than six, then further nonnumerical comparison was made to ascertain the status of the match as valid or not. Approximately 10 percent of the total number of attempted matches fell into this category. To establish computerized procedures for determining which of these possible or marginal cases were actually matches and which were not, a sample of approximately 1,000 such cases were drawn from a preliminary match of 1966 marriages with 1966-1967 births, and these cases were inspected visually for clues as to their matching potential.

It is to be emphasized that the procedure did not involve looking at the actual microfilm record copies (which was done at a later stage of accuracy testing). Rather, the visual inspection involved an attempt to find from the data relationships among variables which ones could aid in the determination of a match.

Since different combinations of variable agreements could develop questionable cases, rules had to be derived to cover each contingency. The first criterion tested was the discrepancy (if any) in the age of the females. Disagreement on this variable, in combination with any other disagreement, could have put this match into the questionable category. If the females' ages, taking into account the time difference in the two events, differed by more than five years in either direction, the match was automatically rejected. A ten-year spread is more than generous, and allows both for some coding error and also for possibility of age misrepresenting on either of the two certificates.

If a match passed this test, it remained in contention as a possible match. The next test referred to the agreement of the middle initial. More confidence can be associated with a disagreement if that disagreement on middle initial arises because there is a blank on one of the two records. If both first and middle initials of the father are blank on the birth certificate and the solicitation code is 1, indicating a probable illegitimate

birth,[1] then the birth match was considered to be incorrect
and was rejected. Furthermore, if neither the male first initials
nor the middle initials agreed, regardless of the disagreement
being due or not due to the presence of blanks, the match was
rejected. However, if the match had survived to this point and
the first initials agreed, but the middle initials disagreed because of the existence of a blank instead of an initial on one of
of the records, the match was accepted.

A final condition tested was that situation in which the male
first initials agreed, but the disagreeing middle initials could
not be ascribed to the presence of a blank. In this case, other
evidence was brought in to see if the match was compelling.
To have survived to this point, the surnames and the female
ages must have been within close agreement. Therefore, if the
county of occurrence agreed and the surname combination was
unique, i.e., there were no other marriage records with that
combination, then the match was accepted. All other cases of
marginal matches were rejected.

Perhaps accuracy is the most important question which
must be handled. Two kinds of errors can be committed when
matching vital records: (1) false positive matches, in which
two records which really do not match are erroneously linked;
and (2) false negative matches, in which two records which do
in fact match are erroneously left unlinked. With respect to
false positive matches, a detailed hand check of 100 computer-
generated linkages showed that for the years 1965-1967, when
fathers' initials were coded for the birth certificates onto the

---

[1] Without requiring a rationale for her request, California law permits
a woman to ask that her having given birth not be made public. This action, which reduces harassment by salespersons, is also used frequently
by mothers of illegitimate children who wish not to publicize the fact of
birth. Using the presence or absence of this information on the birth certificates, the Health Department attempts to determine the reason for a
woman having requested nonsolicitation.

statistical tapes, only 5 percent of the matches were erroneously linked. Unfortunately, time and cost constraints prohibited
a further analysis of the accuracy of the method. No estimate
was made of the extent of false negative matches. The lack of
systematic testing for accuracy is, obviously, a shortcoming
which could prejudice the quality of the data. However, most
cases clearly represented either a match or a nonmatch. Only
10 percent were questionable, and this probably represents
the maximum limit of error.

METHODOLOGY IN SECOND STUDY

The second record linkage undertaken matched marriages
in California in 1966 with births in California in 1966-1967.
While it was structurally the same as the original linkage, the
methodology in the second study differed from the first in
three ways: (1) the way in which the screening variable (surnames) was utilized; (2) the way in which matching weights
were derived; and (3) the way in which threshold values for
accepting or rejecting a match were determined.

The revised methodology was undertaken as an improve-
ment on the original with two goals in mind: (1) increased accuracy; (2) increased generalizability of the matching procedure so that linkages could be replicated for subsequent years.
The revision followed the record linkage model outlined by
Fellegi and Sunter [1969]. Because of the length and com-
plexity of their exposition, I refer the reader to their article
for a clear understanding of the technical aspects of the methodology. I will, however, highlight the difference between the
original and revised methods.

USE OF SCREENING VARIABLES

The first difference between the two methods is actually
unrelated to Fellegi and Sunter's theory. It relates to the use
of surnames as an initial variable for screening out potential

matches from nonmatches. Misspelling is a problem often encountered when using surnames. Precisely because of their relative uniqueness, surnames seem liable to error. A number of schemes have been developed to avoid the tendency of names to be misspelled, the most famous one being the Russell Soundex Code. Under this system the first letter of a surname is kept intact, but all remaining vowels are dropped and subsequent consonants are coded from 0-9 depending upon their falling into certain linear groupings of the consonants in the alphabet. In this way, the basic "sound" of the surname is retained although most vagaries of its spelling are eliminated. The male and female surnames were transformed into Russell Soundex Codes, and these name combinations used for screening. In this way, the exact spelling of the surname became an additional variable of identification which could be examined and given a matching weight. Of 144,085 marriage records coded, the most common Soundex combination occurred 33 times, and 110,372, or 77 percent, were totally unique.

One contribution made by Fellegi and Sunter's theory is the provision of techniques for estimating the frequencies of agreements and disagreements by looking at the joint probabilities of finding particular events in two files, rather than by tedious hand-matching. It is possible, of course, as Newcombe pointed out, to go beyond assigning odds for or against a match simply on the basis of agreement or disagreement. Some items which agree, for example, have different probabilities of agreeing according to their particular properties. In a population of brides, agreement on age 36, which is well into the fourth quartile of ages at marriage in California, is much more likely to indicate a match than agreement on age 18, which occurs much more frequently. Likewise, agreement on father's first initial of 'Y' is more likely to indicate a match than is agreement on the more common initial 'R'. The weights associated with such differential agreements are inversely proportional to the frequency with which they occur in the populations under investigation. Newcombe derived such weights by resorting to hand-matching, whereas Fellegi and Sunter allowed the bypassing of that technique, examining the individual files instead for joint frequencies of occurrence.

The weights are defined as the logarithms of the ratio of the probability of agreement of two variables given that the two records constitute a match, to the probability that agreement is found given that the two records do not constitute a match. Once these probabilities are found for each potential comparison configuration (such as agreement on first initial 'J', or disagreement on age by 6 years) the ratios are calculated, and the logarithm of the ratio is the weight to be assigned such a configuration. Following Fellegi and Sunter, the probabilities are symbolized as follows:

Let m_i^k be the probability of a comparison configuration i for variable k, given a true match.

Let u_i^k be the probability of obtaining comparison configuration i for variable k, given a true nonmatch.

Let $f_{M_i}{}^k$ be the frequency with which configuration i occurs in variable k in file M.

Let $f_{B_i}{}^k$ be the frequency with which configuration i occurs in variable i in file B.

Let N_M and N_B be the total number of records in files M and B, respectively.

Let e_M^k and e_B^k be the probabilities, in files M and B respectively, of variable k being misreported.

Let e_{M0}^k and e_{B0}^k be the probabilities, in Files M and B, respectively, of variable k not being reported.

and

Let e_T^k be the probability that variable k has changed from file M to file B.

Then the probabilities are defined as follows:

$m^k_{i_1}$ (variable k agrees on configuration i)

$$= \frac{f_{Mi}^k + f_{Bi}^k}{N_M + N_B} \; (1-e_B^k)\,(1-e_T)\,(1-e_{MO}^k)\,(1-e_{BO}^k)$$

$m^k_{i_2}$ (variable k disagrees on the two records)

$$= [1-(1-e_M^k)\,(1-e_B^k)\,(1-e_T)]\,(1-e_{MO}^k)\,(1-e_{BO}^k)$$

$m^k_{i_3}$ (variable k not reported on one or both records)

$$= 1-(1-e_{MO}^k)\,(1-e_{BO}^k)$$

$u^k_{i_1}$ (variable k agrees on configuration i)

$$= \frac{f_{Mi}^k}{N_M}\,\frac{f_{Bi}^k}{N_B}\;(1-e_M^k)\,(1-B_B^k)\,(1-e_T)\,(1-e_{MO}^k)$$
$$(1-e_{BO}^k)$$

$u^k_{i_2}$ (variable k disagrees on the two records)

$$= \left[1-(1-e_M^k)\,(1-e_B^k)\,(1-e_T)\sum \frac{f_{Mi}^k}{N_M}\,\frac{f_{Bi}^k}{N_B} \right] x$$
$$x\,(1-e_{MO}^k)\,(1-e_{BO}^k)$$

$u^k_{i_3}$ (variable k not reported on one or both records)

$$= 1-(1-e_{MO}^k)\,(1-e_{BO}^k)$$

The frequencies with which particular configurations occur ($f_{M_i}^k$ and $f_{B_i}^k$) as well as the extent of nonreporting ($e_{B_0}^k$ and $e_{M_0}^k$), can be calculated directly from the two separate files. It might be noted that since $m_{i_3}^k = u_{i_3}^k$, the weight for any comparison in which nonreporting is evident will be zero. Furthermore, in the nature of the records (although not a mathematical necessity) it will be true that $\log(m_{i_1}^k / u_{i_1}^k)$ will yield a positive weight and $\log(m_{i_2}^k / u_{i_2}^k)$ will produce a negative weight.

It should be noted that the extent of missreporting (such as keypunch errors) or variable changes (such as a legal name change or change of residence) is not determined from the files themselves. Because the California Department of Health has a rigorous editing program, the risk of missreporting at that source is low. For other types of missreporting and variable changes no estimates of error level could be determined, and so were ignored. This meant that the values of $e_{M_0}^k$ and $e_{B_0}^k$ were assumed to be zero.

The weights derived for the variables common to marriage and birth records, using the methods outlined above, were used as "look-up" tables in the computer program. It should be noted that prior to assigning a weight for the agreement of surnames, a spelling check was performed. This consisted of matching names letter by letter, and if a mistake was encountered, the computer checked to see if a missing letter on one of the names was the cause of the mistake. If so, agreement was assumed. If not, the mistake was assumed to mean disagreement.

DETERMINING THE THRESHOLD VALUES

Fellegi and Sunter's theory provides for a technique by which the threshold values for a match can be determined on

the basis of the probability of different weights occurring. The
threshold values are those weights (1) mu — above which all
weights signify a true match; and (2) lambda — below which
all weights signify a true nonmatch. If there is middle ground,
then further decision making is necessary. The size of this middle ground is determined by the amount of error the investigator is willing to accept. This error level is specifiable on an a
priori basis. Unfortunately, the method required is complex,
and even after personal communication with Fellegi, the accuracy of the method remains unproved. Communication with
other users of the method confirms the difficulties, and at
this writing, no one to my knowledge has successfully worked
the problem through to completion.

Nonetheless, an initial run of the requisite data (see Fellegi
and Sunter, 1969: 1199-1200 for details) suggested an error

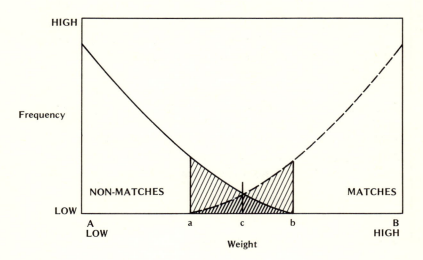

Figure 12
DIAGRAMATIC REPRESENTATION OF THE DISTRIBUTION OF MATCHES
AND NON-MATCHES AND THE CALCULATION OF THRESHOLD VALUES

level of 5 percent, the mu and lambda values converging at a
weight of 6.5, and this weight was taken as a threshold value.
As illustrated by the diagram in Figure 12, most attempted
matches are *clearly* nonmatches or matches. However, the
shaded area under the curve between points "a" and "b,"
where the two distributions overlap, represents the probability
of error which is accepted by choosing a cut-off weight at
point 'C.' More work will be required before it is certain that
the error level was in fact 5 percent. It should be noted that
several editing safeguards were built into the program to ensure
that clearly nonlinkable records were not brought together for
a match. For example, births that were illegitimate (as defined
by the California Department of Health), but which would
had to have occurred after the marriage of the couples in question, were eliminated from consideration. Further, second and
higher matches were checked with previously matched births
to check for consistency of birth dates and recorded mate order,
as well as overall weight, before being added to the record of
a couple. The interested reader can obtain a copy of the complete record linkage computer program from International
Population and Urban Research, University of California,
Berkeley, California 94720.

COMPARISON OF RESULTS FROM FIRST AND SECOND STUDIES

Table 35 presents the numbers of births occurring to women
of a given age at specified intervals after marriage, derived by
each method of record linkage. In general, the comparison re-
veals that the second linkage yielded consistently higher numbers of births than the first linkage. The pattern is for the differences to widen as time after marriage increases. The differences are probably explained by three factors: (1) a decrease
in false negative matches in the second match over the first

Table 35

COMPARISON OF NUMBER OF BIRTHS MATCHED TO WOMEN BY AGE AT MARRIAGE AND TIMING OF FIRST BIRTH: FIRST (1971) AND SECOND (1972) RECORD LINKAGES: CALIFORNIA, 1966

Age at first marriage		Number of births between:	
		0 - 8 Months	8 - 12 Months
15	1971	433	40
	1972	563	86
	Percent Difference	30 Percent	115 Percent
16	1971	1713	338
	1972	2082	527
	Percent Difference	22 Percent	56 Percent
17	1971	2616	579
	1972	3220	972
	Percent Difference	23 Percent	68 Percent
18	1971	3357	1217
	1972	4000	1964
	Percent Difference	19 Percent	61 Percent
19	1971	2606	1019
	1972	3177	1671
	Percent Difference	22 Percent	64 Percent
20	1971	1403	694
	1972	1689	1141
	Percent Difference	20 Percent	64 Percent
21	1971	911	477
	1972	1114	819
	Percent Difference	22 Percent	72 Percent
22-24	1971	1319	826
	1972	1545	1446
	Percent Difference	17 Percent	75 Percent
25+	1971	681	687
	1972	793	1132
	Percent Difference	16 Percent	65 Percent

due to use of Soundex Coding and more precise weighting techniques; (2) an increase in accuracy due to improved sorting of input records prior to the marriage-birth linkage; and (3) in the first study, birth records were, inexplicably, not sorted by birthdate and birth order. That oversight was corrected in the second linkage.

Appendix B

Migration Out of the Record Linkage Framework

The need for estimating the migration out of the record linkage framework arises from the need to have accurate population bases to relate to the incidence of vital events. There are two possible approaches to the problem of this migration. One way would have been to estimate the number of children born (and the timing of such births in relation to marriages) and the incidence of divorce (and its timing) of women who were believed to have migrated out of the record linkage framework and whose vital events after migration were otherwise lost from consideration. The base population would thus always be the full original marriage cohort. Such a procedure involves estimating not only the number of women who have migrated, but also estimating the fertility and marital dissolution levels among these women.

A more practical approach, which minimizes the number of potential estimation errors, is to reduce the population base of the cohort as women are estimated to have left the cohort. This latter approach was adopted for this study. Because of the paucity of both theory and data relating to migration differentials, the somewhat crude estimates of migration which I have derived would lend an air of slight imprecision to the total results even if the record linkage procedure were 100 percent accurate, which it is not. It is my belief, however, that the migration estimates are as accurate as current data permit. The migration data required were age- and marital-duration-specific probabilities of moving out of California during the period 1966-67.

The only available data on migration by age and marital duration for an American population at approximately the right period of time come from the Census Bureau Current Population Surveys on mobility. These data, though limited in detail, provided a starting point. Because the Census Bureau sample sizes at each age were fairly small for any given year, I decided to aggregate the survey data on mobility during the first year of marriage for a five-year period, 1966-1970. These data are summarized in Table 36. Very young (14-17) and very old

Table 36

INTERSTATE MIGRATION OF FEMALES DURING THE FIRST YEAR OF MARRIAGE, BY AGE, AND DURING THE SECOND YEAR OF MARRIAGE: UNITED STATES 1966-1970

Age at survey and year of migration	Total women surveyed	Migrants in year preceding survey	Interstate migrations per 1,000 women
First year			
14-17	504	55	109
18-24	4,527	765	169
25-34	870	116	133
35+	170	17	100
	6,075	954	157
Second year			
	6,841	698	102

Sources: U.S. Bureau of Census (1968, 1969a, 1969c).

(35 and older) brides exhibited the lowest interstate migration rates during the period 1966-1970, while brides aged 18-24 were most prone to move, followed by the brides aged 25-34. Overall, during this period of time, nearly 16 percent of all brides made an interstate move during their first year of marriage. The interstate migration rate dropped to 10 percent on average during the second year of marriage.

Since data by single years of age, at least at the young ages, were required, the interstate migration rates for 1966-1970 for broad age groups were graphed, and interpolations were made by visual inspection for single years of age. The resulting single year of age at first marriage rates of interstate migration during the first year of marriage are presented in Table 37. These data, of course, refer to the population of the entire United States. Although we presumed them to reflect the age pattern of California brides, they were not assumed to measure the absolute rates accurately.

To put migration out of California into perspective with interstate migration for the United States as a whole, reference was made to 1970 census data on outmigration from states. These data relate an individual's residence in 1965 to residence in 1970. By comparing U.S. data on females making an interstate move between 1965 and 1970 with females who migrated out of California during that period of time, we were able to establish a ratio of California outmigration rates to total U.S. mobility by age. These ratios (graphically interpolated between five-year age groups to obtain data for single years of age) are shown in Table 38. Multiplying these ratios by the age-specific migration rates during the first year of marriage for all U.S. women provides a set of estimates of first-year-of-marriage migration rates for California women. These rates are also given in Table 38.

In the absence of data by age, migration rates during the second year of marriage were assumed to follow the same age pattern as during the first year of marriage, but at different levels. In other words, the absolute rates for the first year were multiplied by a constant to obtain the second year rates. Referring again to Table 37, it will be seen that the Current Population Survey data on mobility for the period 1966-70 suggested that interstate mobility during the second year of marriage was at the rate of 102 moves per 1,000 women of all ages. The ratio

Table 37

**COMPARATIVE FIRST YEAR OF MARRIAGE
MIGRATION RATE ESTIMATES:
ALL U.S. FEMALES (1966-1970) AND
1966 CALIFORNIA BRIDES**

Age	(1) U.S. females[a]	(2) California to U.S. ratio[b]	(3) Out-migration of California brides = (1) times (2)
15	109	.95	104
16	109	.92	100
17	109	.89	97
18	130	.87	113
19	150	.84	126
20	169	.81	137
21	164	.78	128
22	159	.75	119
23	154	.75	116
24	149	.77	115
25	144	.78	112
26	139	.80	111
27	135	.82	111
28	131	.85	111
29	128	.88	113
30-34	119	1.02	121
35-39	105	1.00	105
40-44	100	.99	99

[a]Interstate migrations per 1,000 women interpolated graphically from data in U.S. Census [1968, 1969a, 1969c, 1971b].
[b]From U.S. Census [1970b], interpolated graphically for single years of age.

Table 38

ESTIMATING THE DISTRIBUTION OF BRIDES BY RACE (WHITE, NONWHITE), ACCORDING TO AGE: CALIFORNIA MARRIAGE COHORT, 1966

(1)	(2)		(3)		(4)			(5)	(6)	(7)	
	Single women 1966[a]		Probability of marriage during year[b]		Expected distribution of brides = (2) x (3)			Proportion of expected white brides [from (4)] = white/all races	1966 cohort	Estimated cohort racial distribution = (5) x (6)	
Age	Whites	Nonwhites	Whites	Nonwhites	Whites	Nonwhites	All races		All races	Whites	Nonwhites
15	139,348	15,555	.03072	.04365	4,281	679	4,960	.8631	963	831	132
16	132,021	14,031	.06361	.07158	8,398	893	9,291	.9039	5,008	4,527	481
17	125,422	14,510	.10919	.10359	13,695	1,503	15,198	.9011	9,026	8,133	893
18	100,758	11,388	.18499	.14173	18,639	1,614	20,253	.9203	18,026	16,589	1,437
19	79,546	11,006	.21168	.15268	16,838	1,680	18,518	.9093	18,703	17,007	1,696
20	61,128	9,005	.23286	.17679	14,234	1,592	15,826	.8994	12,730	11,449	1,281
21	47,618	7,942	.25988	.18312	12,375	1,454	13,829	.8949	10,749	9,619	1,130
22-24	90,376	14,010	.24018	.18019	21,707	2,524	24,231	.8958	18,611	16,672	1,939
25-29	64,402	11,701	.14824	.13838	9,547	1,619	11,166	.8550	8,579	7,335	1,244
30-34	33,752	5,765	.07540	.09090	2,545	524	3,069	.8293	2,513	2,084	429
35-44	50,519	6,907	.03870	.06038	1,955	417	2,372	.8242	1,860	1,533	327
TOTAL	924,890	121,820	.13430	.11902	124,214	14,499	138,713	.8955	106,768	95,779	10,989

[a]Linear interpolation between 1960 and 1970 census data for California.

[b]Saveland and Glick [1969:247-248]. Data refer to U.S. population 1958-60. Where ages are grouped, the arithmetic mean of single year of age data was calculated.

of second year migration to first year of marriage was thus 0.656. Therefore the migration rates for the second year of marriage were calculated as 0.656 times the rate at each age during the first year.

THE TIMING OF MIGRATION IN RELATION TO THE TIMING OF VITAL EVENTS

Even with migration rates estimated, the task is not complete because more information is still required to estimate the effect of such losses on the California population at risk of a birth or dissolution occurring. It is not known whether couples who moved did so before or after a marital dissolution or a birth of a child. Divorces to California residents occurred outside of California, particularly in Nevada, and were probably more common among women who had been previously married than among those who were dissolving their first marriage. It is also believed that women who migrate tend to have fewer children than those who do not, but little is known of the extent to which a birth or an impending birth may influence a migration decision.

In the light of uncertainty about the timing of a move, it seemed reasonable to assume that removals through migration from the record linkage population were distributed evenly over time. The same assumption would apply to death, but the probability of death in the age groups in question was so low for females that removal by death was ignored. Accounting for deaths would, furthermore, be complicated by the possible duplication of removal by migration followed by death for the same individual. This assumption has varying implications for the period of exposure of migrants to the risk of a vital event, varying in relation to the distribution of vital events. For ex- ample, if all births occurred exactly six months after marriage, then half of the migrants would have been exposed to the risk of childbearing in California and half not. Similarly, if births were distributed evenly throughout the year, then migrants on average would have been exposed to the risk of bearing a child for half a year. However, if, as is empirically the case, all births do not occur at the same time, nor are births distributed evenly over time, then the calculation of the period of exposure becomes more complex.

We can assume, however, that if migration is spread out evenly over an interval of time, then the timing of vital events (births or divorces) will be inversely related to the proportion of migrants exposed to the risk of that event in California. For example, if all births occurred within the first three months of marriage, then at least three-fourths of the migrants would have been exposed to the risk of childbearing before they moved. But, if all births occurred during the last three months of the first year of marriage, then only one-fourth of that year's migrants would have been so exposed. The adjustments for migration out of the record linkage framework were made by (a) multiplying the number of women at the beginning of a year of marriage by the annual migration rates to obtain the total number of migrants during the year; (b) then subtracting migrants from the cohort of women in inverse proportion to the timing of births (or divorces) within the period of time under investigation.

I assumed that total migration (M_1) during any given year (i) after marriage is distributed evenly throughout the year. Thus, the number of women (m_d) migrating out of the record linkage framework during any sub-annual unit of time (d) is as follows:

$$m_d = \frac{d}{365} M_i$$

The timing of births to women of age j during the time interval d will determine the proportion (P_{dj}) of migrants of age j who were at risk of a birth prior to migrating. These women should thus be included in the number of women of age j at risk of a birth during time interval d and are symbolized by w_{dj}. In general, p_{dj} is inversely related to the average (mean) timing of births during interval d or $\overline{b}_{dj}$. Specifically, we assume the following relationship:

$$P_{dj} = 1 - b_{dj}; = b_{dj} = 1$$

The number of women of age j at risk of a birth during the interval $d = d_1 - d_0$ is therefore:

$$w_{dj} = w_{d_0j} - p_{dj}m_{dj}$$

and

$$w_{d_1j} = w_{d_0j} - m_{dj}$$

For purposes of calculation, a few substitutions yield:

$$w_{dj} = w_{d_0j} - (\tfrac{d}{365} M_{ij}) (\overline{b}_{dj})$$

As an example, I will calculate the number of women of age 18 at risk of a birth during the first 6½ months after marriage. The values for each subscript are: $i = 1, j = 18, d_0 = 0, d_1 = 196$, $d = 196$. For this group of brides, the average birth during this interval occurred .628 of the way through the interval (i.e., at 123 days after marriage). Thus, $\overline{b}_{bj} = .666$. There were 18,026 brides of age 18, of whom 11.3 percent, or 2,037 were estimated to have migrated out during the first year of marriage (see Table 39). Thus $M_{ij} = 2,037$, for $i = 1, j = 18$. We now have all the data required to calculate the number of women at risk according to formula (5):

If $j = 18$ and $d = 196$, then

$$w_{dj} = 18,026 - (\tfrac{196}{365} [2,037]) (.666) = 17,298$$

Calculations proceeded similarly for other ages and other time intervals.

It should be kept in mind that references to periods of time are in terms of marriage years and not the calendar year, the two concepts not necessarily being temporally coincident. The marriages of couples in 1966 were, obviously, spread out over the entire calendar year of 1966, so the first (or subsequent) year(s) of marriage is (are) not covered by the same calendar period. Migration during the first year of marriage covered, for example, a period of two calendar years, from January 1966 through December 1967.

Appendix C

ESTIMATION OF THE RACIAL DISTRIBUTION OF BRIDES

The tabulation of California brides in 1966 according to white and nonwhite racial characteristics is employed in Chapter 3. The estimation procedures began with a linear interpolation between the 1960 and 1970 censuses to obtain the distribution of white and nonwhite single women in California in 1966 (see Table 38). Applying a set of age-specific probabilities of marriage to these data produced a hypothetical distribution of brides by race (Table 39). The proportion white at each age was then applied to the cohort of California brides in 1966 to produce the set of distributions of brides by age (Table 39).

To adjust the distribution for migration, migration estimates were made. These involved the assumption that the age pattern of migration was the same for whites and nonwhites, and that only the absolute levels differed. That difference was indexed by the ratio of nonwhite to white outmigration for California between 1965 and 1970 as measured by the 1970 census. These ratios were then applied to the migration rates for the entire cohort to distribute the total number of migrants by race (see Table 39). Calculations then proceeded as discussed in Appendix B.

Table 39

ESTIMATION OF RACIAL DISTRIBUTION OF MIGRANTS OUT OF THE RECORD LINKAGE FRAMEWORK: CALIFORNIA MARRIAGE COHORT, 1966

(1)	(2)	(3)	(4)	(5)	(6)	
Age at first marriage	Total, first year of marriage migrants M_i	Ratio of nonwhite/ total California migration rates 1965-1970[a]	All cohort brides[b]	Nonwhites = (2) x (3)	Racial distribution of brides: Nonwhites = (5) x (6)	Whites = total — nonwhites
			Migration rates for:			
15	100		10.4	3.75	5	95
16	501		10.0	3.60	17	484
17	876	.3605	9.7	3.50	31	845
18	2,037		11.3	4.07	58	1,979
19	2,357		12.6	4.54	77	2,280
20	1,744		13.7	3.20	41	1,703
21	1,376	.2337	12.8	2.99	34	1,342
22-24	2,177		11.7	2.73	53	2,124
25-29	961	.3500	11.2	3.92	49	912
30-34	304	.4800	12.1	5.81	25	279
35-44	190	.3939	10.2	4.02	13	177

[a]From U.S. Bureau of Census [1970b:Table 59].
[b]From Table 37 above; per 100 women.

Appendix D
DEFINING PREMARITAL PREGNANCIES

The first, and to my knowledge the only, review of the literature on premarital pregnancies up to the present is that by Monahan [1960]. Aside from Christensen's studies (see following), little systematic work had been done at the time of Monahan's review, most estimates being derived as spin-offs from other studies. Monahan presented his own set of data, generated from marital and fertility histories of couples seeking marriage counseling at the Domestic Relations Division of the Municipal Court of Philadelphia in 1954. Monahan narrowed down the sample to 3,509 first-marriage families where the wife was a Philadelphia resident. Defining a premarital pregnancy as one which occurred within eight months, fourteen days after marriage, Monahan found that 20 percent of the white women and 46 percent of the black women had been pregnant at the time of marriage.

Although Monahan's study was the first extensive review, the earliest studies devoted to premarital pregnancies were the record linkage studies conducted by Christensen. Among marriages contracted in Utah County, Utah, between 1905 and 1931, 14 percent of the brides aged 20 or younger were apparently pregnant at marriage, as opposed to 8 percent of the brides aged 21 and older [Christensen, 1960]. These figures are not much different from his findings in Tippecanoe County, Indiana, in the 1950s. In Indiana, Christensen discovered that 13 percent of the brides aged 20 and younger were pregnant, compared to 6 percent for those aged 21 and older. In both studies, premarital pregnancies were measured by births within 6½ months after marriage.

One of the most referenced studies of premarital pregnancies, although unpublished, is that done by Pratt [1965] as a doctoral dissertation at the University of Michigan. Pratt's data were drawn from white couples having a first, second, or fourth child in July 1961 in Detroit, and were part of the larger ongoing Detroit Area Study. Data on premarital pregnancies were obtained initially from household interviews, and were then corroborated by a retrospective linkage of marriage and first-birth records. Thus, rather than using record linkage as a primary source of data, a hand search of vital statistics records was done simply as a check on the accuracy of the respondent's information. Pratt then used a two-stage definition of pregnancy. First, following Christensen, Pratt defined a premarital pregnancy as being one which (a) occurred 196 days (6½ months) or less after marriage, or (b) one which occurred between 197 and 265 days but weighed more than 5.5 pounds for a single birth. Using this definition of premarital pregnancy, Pratt found that among his sample of 1,053 fertile white couples in Detroit in 1961, 24.8 percent had been pregnant at marriage.

Another study was done by Lowrie [1965], in which he hand matched marriage, birth, and divorce records in a county in Ohio for the period 1957-1962. Lowrie found that among the 1,850 first marriages that he examined, only 9 percent had pregnancy involvement. Lowrie used births occurring within the first 196 days of marriage as indicating a premarital pregnancy.

A more recent study of premarital pregnancies was done by Whelan [1972a]. Whelan sampled legitimate first births in

Massachusetts during the period 1966-1968, and then looked for marriage records in Massachusetts for the child's parents for the ten-year period preceding the birth. The search for marriages also extended into nearby states. Whelan employed a definition of premarital pregnancies similar but not identical to Pratt's, accepting all births occurring within 196 days as being premaritally pregnant, and accepting those born between 196 and 252 days whose birth weights were in the 90th percentile or higher at the gestational age comparable to their parent's marriage duration. This method was used to attempt to sort out premature births which were postmaritally conceived from premarital conceptions. With this method of obtaining data, and this definition of premarital pregnancies, Whelan found that 24 percent of her white sample, and 38.7 percent of her nonwhite sample brides were pregnant at marriage.

My data, which cover roughly the same period of time as Whelan's, but are for California instead of Massachusetts, show that for the population of women between the ages of 15 and 44 marrying for the first time in 1966, 18 percent of the women were premaritally pregnant, defining a premaritally conceived birth as one which occurred during the first eight months of marriage. I used this definition of premarital pregnancy to achieve some degree of consistency with earlier works, particularly government definitions. For purposes of compatibility, the inclusion of data on birthweight, such as the definition employed by Pratt and by Whelan, result in a level of specificity for which it is difficult to control in most data-gathering situations, and which, while useful for analytic purposes, is not useful for comparative purposes.

References

Acheson, E.D.
    1964   "Oxford Record Linkage Study: A Central File of Morbidity Records for a Pilot Population." *British Journal of Preventive and Social Medicine,* 18: 8-13.

Ashford, J.R., et al.
    1969   "Secular Trends in Late Foetal Death, Neonatal Mortality and Birth Weight in England and Wales 1956-65." *British Journal of Preventive and Social Medicine,* 23(3):154-162.

Ashley, D.J.B.
    1968   "Perinatal Mortality in Wales." *British Journal of Preventive and Social Medicine,* 22(3): 132-137.

Bartz, Karen W. and Nye, F. Ivan
    1970   "Early Marriage: A Propositional Formulation." *Journal of Marriage and the Family,* 32(2): 258-268.

Berkov, Beth
1971   "Illegitimate Births in California: 1966 and
         1967." California Department of Public Health.

1968   "Illegitimate Births in California," *Milbank
         Memorial Fund Quarterly,* 46(4):473-505.

Berkov, Beth and Sklar, June
1972   "An Interim Report on Fertility and Abortion
         in California," Berkeley, International Popula-
         tion and Urban Research (mimeographed ad-
         vance copy).

Becker, Gary S.
1960   "An Economic Analysis of Fertility," in the
         National Bureau of Economic Research,
         *Demographic and Economic Change in
         Developed Countries,* Princeton: Princeton
         University Press.

Blake, Judith
1973   "The Teenage Birth Control Dilemma and
         Public Opinion." *Science,* 180:708-712.

1969   "Population Policy for Americans: Is the
         Government Being Misled?" *Science,* 164:
         522-529.

Brimblecombe, F.S.W. and Ashford, J.R.
1968   "Significance of Low Birth Weight in Perinatal
         Mortality." *British Journal of Preventive and
         Social Medicine,* 22(1):27-35.

Burchinal, Lee G.
1965   "Trends and Prospects for Young Marriages in
         the U.S." *Journal of Marriage and the Family,*
         243-254.

Burgess, Ernest, and Wallis, Paul
    1953   *Engagement and Marriage.* New York:
            John Wiley and Son.

California Department of Public Health
    1971   *Marriage and Divorce in California, 1966-1969.*

Campbell, Arthur A.
    1974   "Beyond the Demographic Transition,"
            Demography, 11(4): 549-561.

Campbell, F.
    1970   "Family Growth and Variation in Family Role
            Structure." *Journal of Marriage and the Family,*
            32(1):45-53.

Cannon, Kenneth and Long, Richard
    1971   "Premarital Sexual Behavior in the Sixties."
            Journal of Marriage and the Family,
            33(1):36-49.

Chase, Helen C. and Nelson, Frieda G.
    1973   "A Study of Risks, Medical Care and Infant
            Mortality," part 3. *American Journal of Public
            Health* 63: supplement, 27-40.

Christensen, H.T.
    1963a   "Timing of First Pregnancy as a Factor in
            Divorce: A Cross-Cultural Analysis."
            Eugenics Quarterly, 10(3):121.

    1963b   "Child-Spacing Analysis via Record Linkage:
            New Data plus a Summing Up from Earlier
            Reports." *Journal of Marriage and Family
            Living,* 25(3):272-280.

    1960   "Cultural Relativism and Premarital Sex Norms."
            American Sociological Review, 25 (1):31-39.

1938   "Rural-Urban Differences in the Time Interval
            Between the Marriage of Parents and the Birth
            of their First Child, Utah County, Utah."
            Rural Sociology, 3(2).

Christensen, H. T. and Gregg, C. F.
  1970   "Changing Sex Norms in America and
              Scandinavia." *Journal of Marriage and
              the Family,* 32(4):616-627.

Cicourel, Aaron
  1974a   *Theory and Method in a Study of Argentine
              Fertility.* New York: Wiley.

  1974b   "Interviewing and Memory," in Colin Cherry,
              ed., *Theory and Decision.* Dordrecht:Reidel.

Cipolla, Carlo M.
  1965   *The Economic History of World Population.*
              Middlesex: Penguin Books.

Coale, Ansley
  1974   "The History of the Human Population."
              Scientific American, 231(3):41-51.

Coombs, Lolagene C. and Freedman, Ronald
  1970   "Premarital Pregnancy, Childspacing, and Later
              Economic Achievement." *Population Studies,*
              24(3):389-412.

Davis, Kingsley
  1973   "The American Family in Relation to Demo-
              graphic Change," in Charles Westoff and
              Robert Parke, Jr., eds., Research Reports of
              the Commission on Population Growth and

the American Future, Vol. 1, *Demographic and Social Aspects of Population Growth* (Washington: Government Printing Office).

1958   "The Early Marriage Trend." *What's New,* 204:2-6.

1939   "Illegitimacy and the Social Structure," *American Journal of Sociology,* 45(2):133-215.

Davis, Kingsley and Blake, Judith
1956   "Social Structure and Fertility: An Analytic Framework." *Economic Development and Cultural Change,* 4(3):211-235.

Day, Richard L.
1967   "Factors Influencing Offspring: Number of Children, Interval Between Pregnancies, and Age of Parents." *American Journal of Diseases of Children,* 113:179-184.

Demos, J.
1968   "Families in Colonial Bristol, Rhode Island, An Exercise in Historical Demography." *William and Mary Quarterly,* 25:40-57.

Donnelly, J.F., Abernathy, J.R., Creadick, R.N., Flowers, C.E., Greenberg, B.G., and Wells, H.B.
1960   "Fetal, Parental, and Environmental Factors Associated with Perinatal Mortality in Mothers Under 20 Years of Age." *American Journal of Obstetrics and Gynecology,* 80(4):663-671.

DuBois, N.S. D'Andrea
1969   "A Solution to the Problem of Linking Multivariate Documents." *Journal of the American Statistical Association,* 64(326):163-174.

Easterlin, Richard A.
    1973   "Does Human Fertility Adjust to the Environ-
                ment?" in Alain Enthoven and A. Myrick
                Freeman, *Pollution, Resources and the Envir-
                onment*. New York: W.W. Norton and Co., Inc.
    1968   *Population, Labor Force, and Long Swings in
                Economic Growth*. New York: National Bureau
                of Economic Research.

Farley, Reynolds
    1970   *Growth of the Black Population*. Chicago:
                Markham Publishing Co.

Farr, William
    1875   Great Britain, *Supplement to the Annual Report
                of the Registrar-General*. London.

Fellegi, Ivan P. and Sunter, Alan B.
    1969   "A Theory for Record Linkage." *Journal of the
                American Statistical Association*, 64(328):
                1183-1210.

Furstenburg, F., Gordis, L. and Markowitz, M.
    1969   "Birth Control Knowledge and Attitudes
                Among Unmarried Pregnant Adolescents:
                A Preliminary Report." *Journal of Marriage
                and the Family*, 31(1):34-42.

Gebhard, Paul
    1971   "Postmarital Coitus Among Widows and
                Divorcees," pp. 81-96 in Paul Bohannon, ed.,
                Divorce and After. Garden City: Doubleday.

George, E.I.
    1973   "Research on Measurement of Family Size
                Norms," in James Fawcett, *Psychological*

Perspectives on Population. New York: Basic Books, pp. 354-370.

Gerard, Marie-Claude and Hemery, Solange
1973   "La Mortalite Infantile en France Suivant le Milieu Social." *Economie et Statistique* 48:33-41.

Glick, Paul and Parke, Robert, Jr.
1965   "New Approaches in Studying the Life Cycle of the Family." *Demography,* 2:187-202.

Goldstein, Sidney
1967   "Premarital Pregnancies and Out-of-Wedlock Births in Denmark, 1950-1965." *Demography,* 4(2):925-936.

Goode, William
1956   *After Divorce.* Glencoe: Free Press.

Great Britain, Registrar-General's Office
1971   *Statistical Review of England and Wales, 1969, part II.* London.

Guralnick, Lillian and Nam, Charles B.
1959   "Census—NOVS Study of Death Certificates Matched to Census Records." *Milbank Memorial Fund Quarterly,* 39(2):144-153.

Hair, P.E.H.
1970   "Bridal Pregnancy in Earlier Rural England further examined." *Population Studies,* 24(1):59-70.

Hartley, Shirley
1969   "Illegitimacy Among 'Married' Women in

England and Wales." *Journal of Marriage and the Family,* 31(4):793-798.

Heady, J.A. and Morris, J.N.
1959 "Social and Biological Factors in Infant Mortality—Variations of Mortality with Mother's Age and Parity." *Journal of Obstetrics and Gynecology of the British Empire,* 66(4):577-592.

Henry, Louis
1961 "Some Data on National Fertility." *Eugenics Quarterly,* 8(2):81-91.

Hoffman, L.W., and Hoffman, M.L.
1973 "The Value of Children to Parents," in James Fawcett, ed., *Psychological Perspectives on Population,* New York: Basic Books.

Institute for Social Research
1974 "Measuring the Quality of Life in America." *ISR Newsletter,* 2(2):Summer.

Israel, S. Leon and Wontersz, Theodore B.
1963 "Teenage Obstetrics—A Comparative Study." *American Journal of Obstetrics and Gynecology,* 85(5):659-668.

Jackson, Edwin
1971 "California's Abortion Legislation and its Demographic Effects," pp. 228-238, in Kingsley Davis and Frederick Styles, editors, *California's Twenty Million.* Institute of International Studies, University of California, Berkeley.

Jacobson, Paul H.
  1959   *American Marriage and Divorce*. New York:
          Rinehart.

Kain, Eugene and Howard, David
  1958   "Postmarital Consequences of Premarital Sex
          Adjustments." *American Sociological Review,*
          23(5):556-562.

Kantner, J. and Zelnick, M.
  1973   "Contraception and Pregnancy: Experience of
          Young Unmarried Women in the U.S.,"
          Family Planning Perspectives, 5(1):21-35.

  1972a   "Sexual Experience of Young Unmarried
          Women in the U.S.," *Family Planning
          Perspectives,* 4(4):9-18.

  1972b   "The Probability of Premarital Intercourse,"
          Social Science Research, 1:335-341.

Kennedy, J.M., Newcombe, H.B. et al.
  1965   *Computer Methods for Family Linkage of
          Vital and Health Records*. Atomic Energy of
          Canada Ltd., AECL-2222.

Keyfitz, Nathan
  1970   "Family Formation as a Probability Process,"
          University of California, Berkeley, unpublished
          ms.

Kitagawa, Evelyn M. and Hauser, Philip M.
  1963   "Methods Used in a Current Study of Social
          and Economic Differentials in Mortality," in
          Milbank Memorial Fund Quarterly, *Emerging
          Techniques of Population Research.*

Knodel, John
   1970   "Two and a Half Centuries of Demographic
               History in a Bavarian Village." *Population
               Studies,* 24(3):353-369.

Krishnan, P. and Kayami, A.
   1974   "Estimates of Age-Specific Divorce Rates for
               Females in the United States, 1960-1969,"
               Journal of Marriage and the Family, 36(1):
               72-75.

Laslett, Barbara
   1973   "The Family as a Public and Private Institution:
               An Historical Perspective." *Journal of Marriage
               and the Family,* 35(3):480-492.

Laslett, Peter
   1965   *The World We Have Lost.* London: Scribners.

Lauriat, Patience
   1969   "The Effect of Marital Dissolution on Fertility."
               Journal of Marriage and the Family, 31(3):
               484-493.

Leibenstein, Harvey
   1957   *Economic Backwardness and Economic Growth.*
               New York: John Wiley and Sons, Inc.

Liebow, Elliot
   1967   *Tally's Corner: A Study of Negro Streetcorner
               Men.* Boston: Little Brown.

Lorenz, Gerda
   1972   "Aspirations of Low-Income Blacks and Whites:
               A Case of Reference Group Processes."
               American Journal of Sociology, 78(2):371-398.

Lowrie, Samuel H.
    1965   "Early Marriage: Premarital Pregnancy and Associated Factors." *Journal of Marriage and the Family*, 27(1):48-56.

McEwan, J.A., Owens, Carol and Newton, J.R.
    1974   "Pregnancy in Girls Under 17: A Preliminary Study in a Hospital District in South London," *Journal of Biosocial Science*, 6:357-381.

Minet, P.L.
    1969   "Fertilite precoce d'une cohorte de mariages dans une province Canadienne." *Acta Genetica et Statistica Medica*, 14(1):186-196.

Monahan, Thomas P.
    1960   "Premarital Pregnancy in the U.S." *Eugenics Quarterly*, 7(3):133-147.

Moss, Joel
    1965   "Teenage Marriages: Cross-National Trends and Sociological Factors in the Decision of When to Marry." *Journal of Marriage and the Family*, 27(2):230-242.

Muhsam, H.V.
    1974   "The Marriage Squeeze." *Demography*, 11(2):291-300.

National Center for Health Statistics (NCHS)
    1974a   "Final Natality Statistics, 1970." *Monthly Vital Statistics Report*, 22(12).

    1974b   "Summary Report, Final Natality Statistics, 1971." *Monthly Vital Statistics Report*, 23(3).

    1973   *Monthly Vital Statistics Report*. 20(5).

1970a   *Monthly Vital Statistics Report.* 18(2).

1970b   *Natality Statistics Analysis,* United States. 1965-1967, Series 21, Number 19.

1968   *Trends in Illegitimacy.* Series 21, Number 15.

1967   *Natality Statistics Analysis.* Report Series 21, Number 11.

1966   *Vital Statistics of the United States.* 1966, Vol. III, Marriage and Divorce.

Newcombe, Howard B.
1967   "Record Linkage: The Design of Efficient Systems for Linking Records into Individual and Family Histories." *American Journal of Human Genetics,* 19(3), part I:335-359.

1965a   "Record Linkage: Concepts and Potentialities." *Mathematics and Computer Science in Biology and Medicine,* London Medical Research Council.

1965b   "Use of Vital Statistics." *United Nations, Proceedings of the World Population Conference, 1965.*

1964   "Pedigrees for Population Studies, A Progress Report." *Cold Spring Harbor Symposia on Quantitative Biology,* 29:21-30.

Newcombe, Howard B. and Smith, Martha E.
1970   "Changing Patterns of Family Growth: The Value of Linked Vital Records as a Source of Data." *Population Studies,* 24(2):193-203.

Newsweek
1974   "Childless Bliss," December 9, 1974.

Pohlman, Edward
1969   *The Psychology of Birth Planning.* Cambridge: Schenkman Publishing Co.

Pratt, William
1965 *A Study of Marriages Involving Premarital Pregnancies.* Unpublished doctoral dissertation, University of Michigan, Department of Sociology.

Presser, Harriet B.
1974 "Early Motherhood: Ignorance or Bliss?" *Family Planning Perspectives,* 6(1):8-14.

Rainwater, Lee
1965 *Family Design: Marital Sexuality, Family Size and Contraception.* Chicago: Aldine.

1960 *And the Poor Get Children.* New York: Quadrangle.

Reiss, Ira L.
1972 "Premarital Sexuality: Past, Present, and Future," in Ira Reiss, ed., *Readings on the Family System.* New York: Holt, Rinehart and Winston, Inc.

Rele, J.R.
1965 "Trends and Differentials in the American Age at Marriage." *Milbank Memorial Fund Quarterly,* 43(2):219-234.

Richards, I.D. Gerald
1972 "Fetal and Infant Mortality Associated with Congenital Malformations." *British Journal of Preventive and Social Medicine.* 27:85-90.

Rindfuss, Ronald, and Westoff, Charles
1974 "The Initiation of Contraception." *Demography,* 11(1):75-87.

Robinson, Derek
1967 "Precedents of Fetal Death." *American Journal of Obstetrics and Gynecology,* 97(7):936-941.

Rotkin, I.D. and King, R.W.
    1962   "Environmental Variables Related to Cervical
              Cancer." *American Journal of Obstetrics and
              Gynecology,* 83(6):720-728.

Russell, C. Scott, et al.
    1968   "Smoking in Pregnancy, Maternal Blood Pres-
              sure, Pregnancy Outcome, Baby Weight and
              growth and other related Factors." *British
              Journal of Preventive and Social Medicine,*
              22(3):119-126.

Ryder, Norman and Westoff, Charles
    1971   *Reproduction in the United States, 1965.*
              Princeton: Princeton University Press.

Saveland, Walt and Glick, Paul
    1969   "First-Marriage Decrement Tables by Color
              and Sex for the United States in 1958-60."
              Demography, 6(1):243-260.

Shah, Farida, Zelnick, Melvin and Kantner, John F.
    1975   "Unprotected Intercourse Among Unwed
              Teenagers." *Family Planning Perspectives*
              7(1):39-44.

Shapiro, S., Schlesinger, E.R. and Nesbitt, E.L., Jr.
    1968   *Infant, Perinatal, Maternal, and Childhood
              Mortality in the United States.* Cambridge:
              Harvard University Press.

Sklar, June and Berkov, Beth
    1974a   "Teenage Family Formation in Postwar
              America." *Family Planning Perspectives,*
              6(2):80-90.

1974b   "Abortion, Illegitimacy, and the American
         Birth Rate." *Science,* 185:909-915.

Smelser, Neil J.
1959   *Social Change in the Industrial Revolution:
         An Application of Theory to the British Cotton
         Industry.* Chicago: Harvard University Press.

Smith, M. Brewster
1973   "A Social-Psychological View of Fertility,"
         in James Fawcett, ed., *Psychological Perspectives
         on Population.* New York: Basic Books.

Stephan, F.F., and McCarthy, P.J.
1958   *Sampling Opinions.* New York: Wiley.

Stewart, Alice M.
1959   "Environmental Hazards of Pregnancy."
         *The Journal of Obstetrics and Gynecology
         of the British Empire,* 66(4):739-742.

Tepping, B.J.
1968   "A Model for Optimum Linkage of Records."
         Journal of the American Statistical Association,
         63:1321-1332.

United Nations
1973a   *Demographic Yearbook, 1971.* New York.

1973b   *National Accounts Statistics Yearbook,*
         1971, Vol. II. New York, United Nations.

United States Bureau of the Census
1974   "Fertility Histories and Birth Expectations of

American Women: June, 1971." *Current Population Reports,* Series P-20, Number 263.

1971a   "Social and Economic Variations in Marriage, Divorce and Remarriage, 1967." *Current Population Reports,* Series P-20, Number 223.

1971b   "Mobility of the Population of the United States: March 1966 to March 1967." *Current Population Reports,* Series P-20, Number 210.

1970a   "Women by Number of Children Ever Born." *Census of Population and Housing,* Subject Reports, PC(2)-3A.

1970b   "Mobility for States and the Nation." *Census of Population and Housing,* Subject Reports, PC(2)-2B.

1969a   "Mobility of the Population of the United States: March 1969 to March 1970." *Current Population Reports,* Series P-20, Number 193.

1969b   "Marriage, Fertility, and Child Spacing." *Current Population Reports,* Series P-20, Number 186.

1969c   "Mobility of the Population of the United States: March 1968 to March 1969." *Current Population Reports,* Series P-20, Number 193.

1968   "Mobility of the Population of the United States: March 1966 to March 1967." *Current Population Reports,* Series P-20, Number 171.

1960   "Women By Number of Children Ever Born." *Census of Population,* 1960, Subject Reports.

1954   "Birth Registration Completeness in the United States, 1950." *Vital Statistics - Special Reports,* 39(2).

1943   "Studies in Completeness of Birth Registration, part I." *Vital Statistics - Special Reports,* 17(18).

Vener, Arthur and Stewart, Cyrus
    1974   "Adolescent Sexual Behavior in Middle America Revisited: 1970-1973." *Journal of Marriage and the Family,* 36(4):728-735.

Vincent, Clark; Harvey, C. Allen; and Cochrane, Carl M.
    1969   "Familial and Generational Patterns of Illegitimacy." *Journal of Marriage and the Family,* 31(4):659-667.

Weeks, John R.
    1975   "Social Psychological Correlates of Fertility Expectations." Paper presented at annual meetings of the Pacific Sociological Association, Victoria, B.C.

    1972   *A Demographic Analysis of Teenage Marriages in California.* Unpublished doctoral dissertation, University of California, Berkeley, Department of Demography.

Whelan, Elizabeth M.
    1972a   "The Temporal Relationship of Marriage, Conception, and Birth in Massachusetts." *Demography,* 9(3):339-414.

    1972b   "Illegitimate and Premaritally Conceived First Births in Massachusetts, 1966-1968." *Social Biology,* 19(2):9-28.

Whelpton, P., Campbell, A. and Patterson, J.
    1966   *Fertility and Family Planning in the United States.* Princeton: Princeton University Press.

Winch, R., McGinnis, R. and Barringer, H.R.
    1962   *Selected Studies in Marriage and the Family.*
            New York: Holt, Rinehart and Winston.

Yaukey, David
    1973   *Marriage Reduction and Fertility.* Lexington:
            D.C. Heath and Co.

Zelnick, Melvin and Kantner, John
    1974   "The Resolution of Teenage First Pregnancies."
            Family Planning Perspectives, 6(2):74-80.

INDEX

ABOUT THE AUTHOR

John R. Weeks, assistant professor of sociology, San Diego State University, has specialized in demographic subjects. He has published in the *Milbank Memorial Fund Quarterly* and is presently at work on the social psychology of fertility behavior.